BEGINNERS'
GERMAN

An Introduction to Conversational German

JOSEPH HARVARD

With Illustrations by
PATRICIA ADAMSON

UNIVERSITY OF LONDON PRESS LTD

Tape recordings of *Beginners' German* are available from the Tutor-Tape Company Ltd, 258 Wimbledon Park Road, London SW19.

Part of the pronunciation practice on pages 91 and 92 has been recorded on a 45 rpm EP record, available from Camera Talks, 31 North Row, London W1. Also available from Camera Talks, is the sequence of filmstrips, *Deutsche Laute*, which will be of interest to teachers. Details are given in the teachers' book, *Teaching Adults to Speak a Foreign Language* (University of London Press Ltd).

ISBN 0 340 08576 2

Sixth impression 1970

University of London Press Ltd
St Paul's House, Warwick Lane, London EC4

Filmset by Keyspools Ltd, Golborne, Lancs
Printed in Great Britain by C. Tinling & Co Ltd.,
Liverpool, London and Prescot

PREFACE

This course is based on considerable practical experience in teaching beginners to speak German. It is essential for a student who wishes to learn the conversational language to study it from the very beginning; moreover as the spoken language is the easiest form of the language, this approach is particularly suitable for all beginners, no matter what their ultimate purpose in learning the language may be.

The ability to speak a language cannot be gained from grammar study or reading, but like any other skill it can be acquired only through systematic and diligent practice. This book provides the material for such practice and presents it in the most suitable way for easy memorising and assimilation.

The lessons in the book have therefore been planned along the following lines. Each lesson begins with a short dialogue which should be thoroughly committed to memory. New words are explained through footnotes on the same page, so that no separate vocabulary is necessary. It will be seen that the great majority of the sentences learnt will serve as models for the formation of numerous other sentences, by the replacement of any word or word-group in the sentence with others of similar structure. This process of substitution is clearly shown in each lesson by the arrangement of several examples of sentence patterns in the form of "substitution tables". These combine several interchangeable word-groups and enable the student to form from them a large number of useful sentences. The student should read aloud as many combinations as possible by taking in turn one entry from each column in the table until all have been completely assimilated and each sentence can be immediately recalled. Only then should the exercises at the end of the book be attempted.

This approach to the learning of a language does not exclude the treatment of grammar. However, grammar itself is not language: it is merely information about it, and when presented, as in this book, after the appearance and practice of each new language form it loses the unpleasant aura which it possesses for many students, and becomes a welcome clarification.

5

In the experience of the author, fluency in any foreign language can be achieved only through practice comparable to—and as necessary as—the finger exercises which must be mastered when learning to play the piano. The method followed in this book ensures that correct expressions only are learnt, and enables the student to proceed confidently from the simple German in the present volume to the more complex forms of expression introduced in the subsequent volumes of the series. These are not merely sequels to *Beginners' German* but also companion books for use in conjunction with it. By its very nature, *Beginners' German* can give only a piecemeal introduction to German grammar, but the second book in the series, *Conversational German*, contains a systematic grammar of the spoken language, as well as a number of useful conversations concerned with foreign travel. Other features of the book are classified lists of the more important idioms for everyday conversation and a great number of sentence-building tables for further fluency practice.

The study of his textbooks will give a student a good basic knowledge of the rudiments of the language. As soon as possible, however, he should start reading some *real* German, i.e. texts written for the enjoyment of German people. The easiest texts, and the most useful from the point of view of the student of the spoken language, are to be found in modern plays and in the dialogues of films. In order to provide a selection of such material a companion book to this course, *German for Pleasure*, has been compiled. Many of the items selected are easy enough for a student to read during his first year of study.

A full explanation of the author's methods and practical advice in the use of the course are given in his *Teaching Adults to Speak a Foreign Language*, which also serves as a Teacher's Book to the series.

In conclusion, the author is greatly indebted to Miss P. Adamson, of Camera Talks, for her charming illustrations, and to Mr. R. S. Kirkman, of the University of London Press Ltd., for his valuable assistance in the preparation of this course.

J.H.

CONTENTS

PRONUNCIATION

German pronunciation, with few exceptions, follows definite rules which, once they are mastered, make it possible for almost every word to be pronounced correctly. The pronunciation indicated here is in accordance with the recognised standard as spoken on the stage or radio. It will be readily understood in all German-speaking countries, although there are considerable variations in different regions. After studying this section, the reader should turn to page 91.

VOWELS

German vowels are pure sounds, i.e. the position of lips, jaws and tongue remains the same throughout whilst the sound is made. This must be borne in mind when consulting the following table. The English equivalents given do not have quite the same sounds, as most English vowels are not pure sounds but diphthongs: e.g. the *o* in h*o*me is pronounced as a mixture of two sounds, something like h*o*-*e*m. The beginner must beware of this and realise that the vowel sounds in German words like *Lohn, Boot, geht, Klee*, are not quite the same as in the English words loan, boat, gate, clay.

A distinction is made between long and short vowels. A vowel is long:

(1) when doubled: *Aal, Tee, Boot*.

(2) when followed by *h*: *Bahn, Sohn, Uhr*.

(3) when followed by one consonant only: *gut, Hof, Tal*.

(4) before a single consonant followed by a vowel: *Leben, Name, Rose*.

A vowel is short when followed by more than one consonant: *Bett, warten, Milch*.

The vowel *e* is short in the endings *-e, -el, -en, -er*: *Gabe, Gabel, Garten, Fenster*.

SPELLING	PRONUNCIATION	EXAMPLES
ah ⎫		der Hahn, *rooster*
aa ⎬ like the *a* in *father*		der Aal, *eel*
a long ⎭		das Tal, *valley*

8

SPELLING	PRONUNCIATION	EXAMPLES
a short	the same, but much shorter	der Mann, *man* der Gast, *guest* die Hast, *haste*
eh *ee* *e* long	like the *a* in *taste*	mehr, *more* der Klee, *clover* der Esel, *donkey*
e short	as in *get*	die Welt, *world*
ie *ih* *ieh*	like the *ie* in *field*	das Tier, *animal* ihr, *her* das Vieh, *cattle*
i short	as in *sin*	das Kind, *child*
oh *oo* *o* long	similar to the *o* in *note* but no diphthong and spoken with rounded lips	der Sohn, *son* das Boot, *boat* rot, *red*
o short	as in *hot*	die Motte, *moth*
uh *u* long	as in *rude*	der Stuhl, *chair* der Bruder, *brother*
u short	as in *put*	die Butter, *butter*

MODIFIED VOWELS

These are *ä*, *ö*, *ü*, *äu*, and they are pronounced differently from *a*, *o*, *u*, *au*.

äh *ä* long	like the *a* in *fate*	während, *during* spät, *late*
ä short	like the *e* in *net*	die Wände, *walls*
öh *ö* long	like no English sound. It is the same sound as French *eu* in *deux* (pronounced by saying "day" with rounded lips).	die Söhne, *sons* hören, *hear*
ö short	like *i* in *sir*	göttlich, *divine*

9

SPELLING	PRONUNCIATION	EXAMPLES

üh ⎫
ü long ⎭ — like no English sound. It is the same sound as French *u* in *tu* (pronounced by saying "tea" with rounded lips).

die kühn, *bold*
die Blüte, *bloom*

ü short — the same as above, only shorter, i.e. the *i* in "miller" spoken with rounded lips.

füllen, *to fill*
der Müller, *miller*

äu — see below under "Diphthongs"

DIPHTHONGS

There are only three diphthongs in German, and they are always long.

au	like *ou* in *house*	die Frau, *woman*
eu ⎫ *äu* ⎭	like *oy* in *toy*	die Leute, *people* die Bäume, *trees*
ei ⎫ *ai* ⎬ *ay* ⎭	like *ei* in *height*	das Ei, *egg* der Kaiser, *emperor* Bayern, *Bavaria*

CONSONANTS

These are pronounced as in English with the following exceptions:

b	as in English, but like *p* if followed by another consonant or at the end of a word	das Buch, *book* das Obst, *fruit* das Grab, *grave*
d	as in English, but like *t* at the end of a word	der Dieb, *thief* das Land, *land*
ch	like the *h* in *huge* or *Hugo*; after *a, o, u, au*, as in Scottish *loch*	die Milch, *milk* das Loch, *hole* auch, *also*
chs	like *x*	der Ochse, *ox* sechs, *six*

10

SPELLING	PRONUNCIATION	EXAMPLES
g	as in *go*; at the end of a word, like *k*	gut, *good* der Ring, *ring*
j	like *y* in *yes*	jung, *young*
l	as in *lamp*; never as in *all*	die Lampe, *lamp* alles, *all*
r	Of the various *r* sounds used by different speakers we recommend the so-called uvular *r*, which is the most commonly used. It is produced at the back of the mouth (like the hard *g*) and may be practised by saying repeatedly: *Gabe, grabe, Rabe; Gott, rot; gut, Ruth.* It is in fact the sound which we produce repeatedly when gargling, and is not difficult to acquire.	die Rose, *rose* der Rabe, *raven* graben, *to dig* rot, *red*
s	before and between vowels, as in *wise* before consonants and at the end of a word, as in *son* in the combinations *sp* and *st* at the beginning of a word or syllable, like English *sh*	der Sohn, *son* der Rasen, *lawn* der Geist, *ghost* das Gras, *grass* das Spiel, *game* der Stuhl, *chair* die Gestalt, *shape*
ss	always like sharp *s* as in *son*	das Wasser, *water*
ß	is a special sign for sharp *s*, indicating that the preceding vowel is long. It is always used instead of *ss* at the end of a word.	die Straße, *street* naß, *wet*
sch	like English *sh*	das Schiff, *ship*
th	like *t*	der Thron, *throne*

11

SPELLING	PRONUNCIATION	EXAMPLES
v	like English f	der Vater, *father*
w	like English v	der Wagen, *car*
z } tz }	like *ts* in *its*	der Zucker, *sugar* die Katze, *cat*

Double consonants are pronounced like single ones, except in compound words, where they are sounded separately: *ab/brechen*, to break off; *an/nehmen*, to accept.

Exceptional Pronunciations

(1) Although followed by more than one consonant, the vowel is long in: *Adler, Buche, Erde, erst, Herd, Herde, Husten, Kloster, Kuchen, Ludwig, Mond, nächste, Papst, Pferd, Obst, Ostern, Österreich, Schuster, Schwert, Sprache, Städte, stets, suchen, werden, wert, wusch, Wüste.*

(2) Although followed by one consonant only, the vowel is short in: *ab, am, an, das, es, hat, man, ob, um, von, weg, zum, Grog.*

(3) *i* is long in: *Tiger, Bibel, Fibel, fidel, Figur, Rosine, Mandoline, Kusine*, and other words ending in *-ine*.

(4) *g* and *j* are pronounced in the French way (i.e. like the *s* in *pleasure*) in: *Loge, Page, Gelee, Jackett, Journalist.*

(5) *i* and *e* are pronounced separately in: *Familie, Lilie, Aktie, Patient, Bankier, Portier* (the last two are pronounced in the French way).

(6) *Café** and *Restaurant* are pronounced as in French.

(7) Each *e* is sounded separately in *Museen* (the plural of *das Museum*) and *Seen* (the plural of *der See*, lake).

(8) *-ig* at the end of a word is pronounced as if spelled *-ich*: *neblig, völlig, gütig, rüstig*, etc.

(9) *v* in words of foreign origin is pronounced like English *v*: *November, nervös, Nerven.*

* Distinguish between *der Kaffee*, the drink, and *das Café* the place.

The Glottal Stop

Whereas in French and English the final consonant of a word is often joined on in pronunciation to the next word if the latter begins with a vowel, this is not so in German. There must be a complete break between the words—the so-called "glottal stop": *Er / ist / ein alter / Esel.*

This stop is also made in the middle of a word: *uninteressant,* although written as one word, is pronounced *un/interessant.*

Stress

The first syllable of a word is stressed, except in:

(1) Words beginning with *be-, ge-, emp-, ent-, er-, ver-, zer-,* which take the stress on the second syllable.

(2) Da*mit,* da*rauf,* wo*hin,* wo*raus,* hi*nauf,* her*ein* and other compounds with *da, wo, hin* and *her,* all of which are stressed on the second syllable.

(3) buch*stäb*lich, all*mäh*lich, ab*scheu*lich, vor*treff*lich, vor*züg*lich, le*ben*dig, Ber*lin,* Stet*tin,* Bay*reuth,* Hann*o*ver, West*fa*len.

(4) Many words of foreign origin, which retain their original stress: das H*o*tel, das Mus*e*um, die Mu*sik,* das Pa*pier,* die Kra*wa*tte, der Offi*zier,* der Pro*fes*sor, die Peri*o*de, die Stu*dent,* die Stu*den*tin, das Para*dies,* der Dia*mant,* die Mando*li*ne, die Ku*si*ne, die Ro*si*ne, der Pro*zeß,* der Rheuma*tis*mus, das Rhinozeros, die Na*tion,* die Revolu*tion,* das Regi*ment,* der Gener*al,* der Sol*dat,* Ap*ril,* Au*gust,* Sep*tem*ber, Ok*to*ber, No*vem*ber, De*zem*ber, ele*gant,* intelli*gent,* interes*sant,* pri*vat* and many others.

In compounds the main stress falls on the first part: der *Blei*stift, die *Füll*feder, das *Wör*terbuch.

The second part is stressed in: das Jahr*zehnt,* das Jahr*hund*ert, Großbri*tan*nien, Ober*am*mergau, voll*kom*men, will*kom*men, ausge*zeich*net, augen*blick*lich.

Both parts are equally stressed in compounds expressing a comparison: *bildschön, saudumm, totenstill.*

Longer compounds may have more than one stressed syllable. *Stra*ßenbahn*wa*gen, *Un*tergrundbahnsta*tion,* *Ak*tienge*sell*schaft, Zigar*et*tenfa*briks*direktor, *Schorn*steinfegerge*sang*ver*ein.*

INTONATION

The way in which the voice rises and falls in connected speech cannot be learned from a book. It is best learned in the same way as a new tune: by hearing it repeatedly and then trying to imitate it.

CAPITAL LETTERS

Initial capital letters are used for all nouns, as well as adjectives and verbs used as nouns: *der Garten, die Alte, das Lesen und Schreiben.*

National adjectives have small initial letters, unless they form part of a geographical designation: *meine deutschen Freunde, englisches Geld, spanische Briefmarken*: but *die Deutsche Bundesrepublik.* Note also: *das Schwarze Meer, die Vereinigten Staaten.*

GOTHIC TYPE

Roman type is now used everywhere in German-speaking countries, so that it is unnecessary to teach the Gothic alphabet in a beginners' book. Most books and newspapers are now printed in roman type. To be able to read books printed before the war, the advanced student will require some familiarity with Gothic type. It is not very difficult to read. Examples of Gothic type are given in *German for Pleasure*, the reader which accompanies this course.

THE ALPHABET

LETTER	PRONUNCIATION	LETTER	PRONUNCIATION
a	*ah*	*n*	*enn*
b	*bay*	*o*	*oh*
c	*tsay*	*p*	*pay*
d	*day*	*q*	*koo*
e	*ay*	*r*	*airr*
f	*eff*	*s*	*ess*
g	*gay*	*t*	*tay*
h	*hah*	*u*	*oo*
i	*ee*	*v*	*fow*
j	*yott*	*w*	*vay*
k	*kah*	*x*	*iks*
l	*ell*	*y*	*ip-see-lon*
m	*emm*	*z*	*tset*

The modified vowels *ä, ö, ü* (for pronunciation see pages 9 and 10) are called *a Umlaut, o Umlaut, u Umlaut*. *ss* is called *ess ess* or *doppel ess*. *ß* is called *ess tset* (for pronunciation see page 11).

NUMERALS

CARDINAL		ORDINAL[1]	
			der (die, das)
1	eins	1st	erste
2	zwei	2nd	zweite
3	drei	3rd	dritte
4	vier	4th	vierte
5	fünf	5th	fünfte
6	sechs	6th	sechste
7	sieben	7th	siebente
8	acht	8th	achte
9	neun	9th	neunte
10	zehn	10th	zehnte
11	elf	11th	elfte
12	zwölf	12th	zwölfte

[1] These are adjectives and take different endings according to the rules given on pp. 38 and 42.

13	dreizehn	13th	dreizehnte
14	vierzehn	14th	vierzehnte
15	fünfzehn	15th	fünfzehnte
16	sechzehn	16th	sechzehnte
17	siebzehn	17th	siebzehnte
18	achtzehn	18th	achtzehnte
19	neunzehn	19th	neunzehnte
20	zwanzig	20th	zwanzigste
21	einundzwanzig	21st	einundzwanzigste
22	zweiundzwanzig	22nd	zweiundzwanzigste
23	dreiundzwanzig	23rd	dreiundzwanzigste
30	dreißig	30th	dreißigste
40	vierzig	40th	vierzigste
50	fünfzig	50th	fünfzigste
60	sechzig	60th	sechzigste
70	siebzig	70th	siebzigste
80	achtzig	80th	achtzigste
90	neunzig	90th	neunzigste
100	hundert	100th	hundertste
101	hunderteins	101st	hunderterste
102	hundertzwei	102nd	hundertzweite
103	hundertdrei	103rd	hundertdritte
200	zweihundert	200th	zweihundertste
1000[1]	tausend	1000th	tausendste
10000[1]	zehntausend	10000th	zehntausendste
100000	hunderttausend	100000th	hunderttausendste
1000000	eine Million	1000000th	Millionste
2000000	zwei Millionen	2000000th	zwei Millionste

FRACTIONS		DECIMALS
$\frac{1}{2}$ = ein halb[2]	0,5	= Null Komma fünf
$\frac{1}{4}$ = ein Viertel	0,25	= Null Komma zwei fünf
$\frac{3}{4}$ = drei Viertel	1,1	= Eins Komma eins
$\frac{1}{3}$ = ein Drittel	1,01	= Eins Komma null eins
$\frac{3}{8}$ = drei Achtel	1,001	= Eins Komma null null eins

[1] *These may be written* '1.000', '10.000' *etc., but not with a comma, which is used to indicate decimals.*

[2] halb *is an adjective. The corresponding noun is* die Hälfte.

Lektion Eins

Kommen Sie herein!

Nehmen Sie Platz!

Rauchen Sie?

Sie trinken eine Tasse
Kaffee, nicht wahr?

Nehmen Sie Milch?

Nehmen Sie Zucker?

17

BITTE SEHR!

A: Rauchen Sie?*

B: Danke,[1] ich rauche nicht.[2]

A: Sie trinken eine Tasse Kaffee,* nicht wahr?[E]

B: Danke gern.[3]

A: Nehmen Sie Milch?*

B: Ein wenig,[4] bitte.[5]

A: Zucker?*

B: Ein Stück,[6] bitte.

A: Bitte sehr.[7]

B: Danke schön.[8]

[1] danke *or* nein, danke, *no thank you.*
[2] ich rauche nicht, *I don't smoke.*
[3] danke gern, *thank you (when accepting; lit. "thanks gladly").*
[4] ein wenig, *a little.*
[5] *please.*
[6] ein Stück, *one piece.*
[7] bitte sehr *is said when handing something.*
[8] danke sehr *or* danke schön, *thank you very much.*

ABBREVIATIONS *used throughout the lessons:*

*: see Illustrations.
[F]: see Fluency Practice.
[E]: see Explanations.

m.: masculine.
f.: feminine.
pl.: plural.

FLUENCY PRACTICE

1. Kommen Sie!
   Warten Sie!
   Hören Sie!
   Lesen Sie das!
   Halten Sie das!

   Come.
   Wait.
   Listen.
   Read that.
   Hold that.

2. Kommen Sie, bitte!
   Warten Sie, bitte!
   Lesen Sie das, bitte!
   Halten Sie das, bitte!
   Schreiben Sie das bitte auf!

   Please come.
   Please wait.
   Please read that.
   Please hold that.
   Please write that down.

3. Kommen Sie doch!
   Warten Sie doch!
   Essen Sie doch!
   Trinken Sie doch!
   Hören Sie doch!
   Lesen Sie das doch bitte!
   Schreiben Sie das doch bitte auf!

   Do come.
   Do wait.
   Do eat.
   Do drink.
   Do listen.
   Please do read that.
   Please do write that down.

18

4. Warten Sie nicht!	*Don't wait.*
Gehen Sie nicht!	*Don't go.*
Lesen Sie das nicht!	*Don't read that.*
Sagen Sie das nicht!	*Don't say that.*
Schreiben Sie das bitte nicht auf!	*Please don't write that down.*
Sprechen Sie bitte nicht so schnell!	*Please don't speak so fast.*
Sprechen Sie langsam!	*Speak slowly.*
Sprechen Sie bitte langsamer!	*Please speak more slowly.*
5. Sie kommen, nicht wahr?	*You are coming, aren't you?*
Sie warten, nicht wahr?	*You are waiting, aren't you?*
Sie sprechen deutsch, nicht wahr?	*You speak German, don't you?*
Sie verstehen, nicht wahr?	*You understand, don't you?*

EXPLANATIONS

1. The Imperative (i.e. the form of a verb expressing a command or request) ends in *-en*, and the word *Sie* (spelt with a capital *S*) is added.

2. Any form of the verb used in connection with *Sie*, you, ends in *-en*, e.g. *Sie kommen*, you are coming; *Kommen Sie?* Are you coming?; *Kommen Sie!* Come!; *Kommen Sie nicht!* Don't come!

3. The distinction made in English between 'you smoke' and 'you are smoking' is not made in German. *Sie rauchen* stands for both. Similarly, *Sie sprechen deutsch, nicht wahr?* means both 'you speak German, don't you?' and 'you are speaking German, aren't you?'

4. The addition of *nicht*, not, provides the negative form of the verb. *Sie essen nicht* stands for both 'you don't eat' and 'you are not eating'.

5. *Doch* added to a command or request makes it more emphatic, e.g. *Schreiben Sie doch!* Do write.

6. *Nicht wahr?* is short for *Ist es nicht wahr?* Is it not true? Like the French *N'est-ce pas?* it is the equivalent of 'Aren't you? Isn't it? Don't you? Doesn't he? Haven't you? Hasn't he?' etc.

Lektion Zwei

das Bier

die Flasche
(eine Flasche Wein)

die Milch

der Krug
(ein Krug Bier)

der Wein

das Glas
(ein Glas Milch)

WAS TRINKEN SIE?

A: *Der Herr*.   B: *Die Dame*.   C: *Der Kellner*.[1]

A: Was trinken Sie?[F]

B: Ich trinke eine Tasse Schokolade.

A: Was essen Sie?[F]

B: Ich esse ein Schinkenbrot.[2]

A: Herr Ober!—Eine Tasse Schokolade und ein Schinkenbrot für
die Dame, und für mich[3] ein Glas Bier und ein Käsebrot.[4]

[1] der Kellner, *the waiter* (*usually
called* Herr Ober).
[2] der Schinken, *ham*; das Schinkenbrot,
ham sandwich.

[3] *me*.
[4] der Käse, *cheese*.

20

C: Edamer[1] oder Tilsiter[1] Käse?

A: Edamer, bitte.

B: Die Schokolade ist gut.

A: Das Bier ist auch[2] gut. Es ist eiskalt.

B: Der Schinken ist gut.

A: Der Käse ist auch nicht schlecht.[3]

A: Ober, die Rechnung[4] bitte.[5]

C: Drei[6] Mark, bitte.

[1] *kinds of cheese.*
[2] *also.*
[3] *bad.*
[4] die Rechnung, *bill.*
[5] *please.*
[6] *three.*

FLUENCY PRACTICE

1. Kommen Sie?   *Are you coming?*
   Gehen Sie?   *Are you going?*
   Warten Sie?   *Are you waiting?*
   Sehen Sie das?   *Do you see that?*
   Sprechen Sie deutsch?   *Do you speak German?*
   Lesen Sie jetzt?   *Are you reading now?*

2. Ja, ich komme.   *Yes, I am (coming).*
   Ja, ich gehe.   *Yes, I am (going).*
   Ja, ich warte.   *Yes, I am (waiting).*
   Ja, ich sehe das.   *Yes, I do (see that).*
   Ja, ich spreche deutsch.   *Yes, I do (speak German).*
   Ja, ich lese jetzt.   *Yes, I am (reading now).*

3. Nein, ich komme nicht.   *No, I am not (coming).*
   Nein, ich gehe nicht.   *No, I am not (going).*
   Nein, ich warte nicht.   *No, I am not (waiting).*
   Nein, ich sehe das nicht.   *No, I don't (see that).*
   Nein, ich spreche nicht deutsch.   *No, I don't (speak German).*
   Nein, ich lese jetzt nicht.   *No, I am not (reading now).*

4. Kommen Sie nicht?   *Aren't you coming?*
   Gehen Sie nicht?   *Aren't you going?*
   Warten Sie nicht?   *Aren't you waiting?*
   Sehen Sie das nicht?   *Don't you see that?*
   Essen Sie nicht?   *Aren't you eating?*
   Trinken Sie nicht?   *Aren't you drinking?*

21

5. Doch,[E] ich komme. Yes, I am (coming).
   Doch, ich gehe. Yes, I am (going).
   Doch, ich warte. Yes, I am (waiting).
   Doch, ich sehe das. Yes, I do (see that).
   Doch, ich esse. Yes, I am (eating).
   Doch, ich trinke. Yes, I am (drinking).

6. Was trinken Sie? What are you drinking? What do you drink?

Ich trinke			
	Tee.	I drink	tea.
	Kaffee.	I am drinking	coffee.
	Kakao.		cocoa.
	Milch.		milk.
	Wasser.		water.
	Bier.		beer.
	Wein.		wine.

7. Was essen Sie? What are you eating? What do you eat?

Ich esse			
	ein Käsebrot.	I eat	a cheese sandwich.
	ein Schinkenbrot.	I am eating	a ham sandwich.
	ein Wurstbrot.		a sausage sandwich.
	ein Stück Schokolade.		a piece of chocolate.
	Fleisch mit Gemüse.		meat with vegetables.
	Fisch mit Salat.		fish with salad.
	Erdbeereis.		strawberry ice-cream.

8.

Der	Fisch	ist	gut.	The	fish	is	good.
	Käse	ist nicht	schlecht.		cheese	is not	bad.
	Kaffee				coffee		
Die	Wurst			The	sausage		
	Milch				milk		
	Butter				butter		
Das	Brot			The	bread		
	Fleisch				meat		
	Wasser				water		

9.

Da	ist	der	Wagen.	There	is	the	car.
Dies		ein	Bahnhof.	This		a	station.
Das			Chauffeur.	That			driver.
		die	Tür.			the	door.
		eine	Tasse.			a	cup.
			Wurst.				sausage.
		das	Käsebrot.			the	cheese sandwich.
		ein	Glas Bier.			a	glass of beer.
			Gemüse.				vegetable.

22

1. *Der* = the, before a masculine noun.

   Die = the, before a feminine noun.

   Das = the, before a neuter noun.

In grammar *masculine* and *feminine* do not mean *male* and *female*. as in German all nouns (whether names of persons or things) belong to one of the three groups: masculine, feminine, neuter.

2. *Ein* = a (an), before masculine and neuter nouns.

   Eine = a (an), before a feminine noun.

3. The form of the verb used in connection with *ich* (I) ends in -*e*.

4. There is no difference in German between 'Are you reading?' and 'Do you read?' Both forms are expressed by *Lesen Sie?*

5. In answer to a negative question *doch* is more emphatic than *ja*. For further emphasis both together may be heard: *Ja doch!* 'Yes, indeed! Of course!' whereas *Nicht doch!* means 'Certainly not! Oh no!'

Lektion Drei

Herr Fischer, der Vater:
er liest die Zeitung.

Frau Fischer, die Mutter:
sie kocht das Mittagessen.

Hans, der ältere Sohn:
er liest ein Buch.

Lotte, die ältere Tochter:
sie spielt Tennis.

Fritz, der jüngere Sohn:
er spielt Ball.

Grete, die jüngere Tochter:
sie ißt ein Eis.

DIE FAMILIE

A: *Er.*   B: *Sie.*

A: (*zeigt*[1] *Photographien*): Dies[2] ist mein[E] Vater* und das[3] ist
    meine[E] Mutter.*

B: Ihr[E] Vater ist groß,[4] nicht wahr?

A: Ja, er[F] ist groß und dick.[5]

B: Ihre[E] Mutter ist nicht so groß wie Ihr Vater.

A: Sie[F] ist viel[6] kleiner.[7]

B: Ist die junge Dame Ihre ältere* Schwester?

A: Ja, das ist sie.

B: Sie ist groß und schlank,[8] nicht wahr?

A: Ja. Sie spielt* viel Tennis.

B: Dies ist Ihr Bruder,[F] nicht wahr?

A: Ja, das ist der älteste.[E]

B: Wer[9] ist der Knabe?[F]

A: Auch[10] mein Bruder.

B: Wie[11] heißt[12] er?

A: Er heißt Fritz.

B: Wie alt ist er?

A: Er ist zehn[13] Jahre alt.

B: Wer ist das Mädel?[14]

A: Meine Schwester.[F] Sie heißt Grete.

B: Wie alt ist sie?

A: Sie ist neun.[15]

B: Wo[16] sind Sie?

A: Ich photographiere.

---

[1] *shows.*
[2] *this.*
[3] *that.*
[4] *tall.*
[5] *stout.*
[6] *much.*
[7] *smaller.*
[8] *slim.*

[9] *who.*
[10] *also.*
[11] *how.*
[12] *is called*
[13] *ten.*
[14] *girl.*
[15] *nine.*
[16] *where.*

1.

Der Mann	kommt	jetzt (nicht).		*The man*	*is (not)*	*coming*	*now.*
Er	geht			*He*		*going*	
	wartet					*waiting*	
Die Frau	spielt			*The woman*		*playing*	
Sie	ißt			*She*		*eating*	
	trinkt					*drinking*	
Das Kind	schreibt			*The child*		*writing*	
Es	liest			*It*		*reading*	

2.

Kommt	der Mann	jetzt (nicht)?		*Is(n't)*	*the man*	*coming*	*now?*
Geht	er				*he*	*going*	
Wartet						*waiting*	
Spielt	die Frau				*the woman*	*playing*	
Ißt	sie				*she*	*eating*	
Trinkt						*drinking*	
Schreibt	das Kind				*the child*	*writing*	
Liest	es				*it*	*reading*	

3.

Ja,	er	kommt	jetzt (nicht).		*Yes,*	*he*	*is (not)*	*coming*	*now.*
Doch,[1]	sie	geht			*Yes,*[1]	*she*		*going*	
(Nein,)	es	ißt			*(No,)*	*it*		*eating*	
		spielt						*playing*	
		liest						*reading*	

[1] *In answer to a negative question.*

4.

Da	ist	mein	Vater.		*There*	*is*	*my*	*father.*
Das		Ihr	Bruder.		*That*		*your*	*brother.*
Dies			Sohn.		*This*			*son.*
			Mann.					*husband.*

		meine	Mutter.				*my*	*mother.*
		Ihre	Schwester.				*your*	*sister.*
			Tochter.					*daughter.*
			Frau.					*wife.*

		mein	Kind.				*my*	*child.*
		Ihr	Eis.				*your*	*ice-cream.*
			Bier.					*beer.*
			Fleisch.					*meat.*

5.

Ißt	Ihr	Mann	Fleisch?		*Does your*	*husband*	*eat*	*meat?*
		Vater	Fisch?			*father*		*fish?*
		Sohn	Wurst?			*son*		*sausage?*
		Kind	Schinken?			*child*		*ham?*
			Käse?					*cheese?*
	Ihre	Frau	Obst?			*wife*		*fruit?*
		Mutter	Kuchen?			*mother*		*cake?*
		Schwester	ein Butterbrot?			*sister*		*a slice of*
		Tochter				*daughter*		*bread and butter?*
			eine Apfelsine?					*an orange?*

6.
Ja,	er	ißt das (ißt das nicht).	Yes,	he	eats that (doesn't eat
(Nein,)	sie		(No,)	she	that).
	es			it	

7.
Mein Mann	trinkt	Tee.	My husband	drinks	tea.
Er		Kaffee.	He		coffee.
		Kakao.			cocoa.
Meine Frau		Milch.	My wife		milk.
Sie		Wasser.	She		water.
		Limonade.			lemonade.
Mein Kind		Bier.	My child		beer.
Es		Wein.	It		wine.

8.
Was	ist das?	What	is that?
	essen Sie?		are you eating? or do you eat?
	trinken Sie?		are you drinking? or do you drink?
	ißt Ihr Mann?		is your husband eating? or does . . . eat?
	trinkt Ihre Frau?		is your wife drinking? or does . . . drink?

9.
Wer ist	der Knabe?	Who is	the boy?
Wie heißt	das Mädel?	What is the name of	the girl?
Wie alt ist	der alte Herr?	How old is	the old gentleman?
Wo schläft	die junge Dame?	Where sleeps	the young lady?
	das kleine Kind?		the little child?

EXPLANATIONS

1. Mein, *my* ⎱ before masculine and neuter nouns in the
   Ihr, *your* ⎰ singular.

   Meine, *my* ⎱ before feminine nouns in the singular and all
   Ihre, *your* ⎰ nouns in the plural.

2. When expressing what he, she or it does (*or* is doing), the verb ends in *-t*.

3. Note the change of vowel occurring in some verbs:

ich esse	Sie essen	er (sie, es) ißt
ich lese	Sie lesen	er (sie, es) liest
ich schlafe	Sie schlafen	er (sie, es) schläft

4. Distinguish between *ist*, is, and *ißt*, eats. There is no difference in pronunciation.

5. der (die, das) ältere, *the elder*
   der (die, das) jüngere, *the younger*
   der (die, das) älteste, *the eldest*
   der (die, das) jüngste, *the youngest*

Lektion Vier

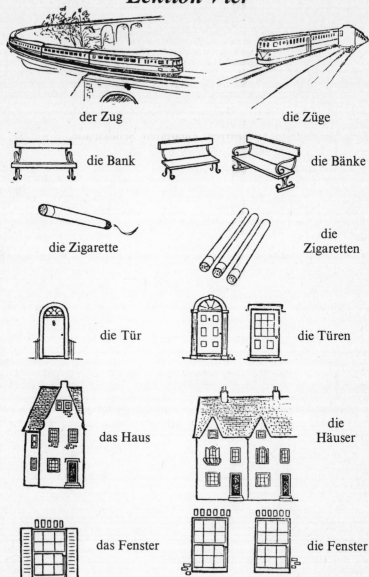

der Zug

die Züge

die Bank

die Bänke

die Zigarette

die Zigaretten

die Tür

die Türen

das Haus

die Häuser

das Fenster

die Fenster

28

Im Zug (1)

(*Die Familie Fischer ist im Zug[1] von[2] Hamburg nach[3] Berlin. Herr Fischer liest eine Zeitung. Frau Fischer liest ein Buch. Eine andere[4] Dame (Frau Schulz) strickt.[5] Die Kinder schauen[6] durch[7] das Fenster. Ein Herr liest[F] eine englische Zeitung.*)

Ein Reisender[8]: Ist hier ein Platz[F] frei?

Herr Fischer: Nein, alle Plätze[F] sind besetzt.[9]

Ein Verkäufer[10]: Zeitungen, Zeitschriften,[11] Bücher.

Eine Verkäuferin[12]: Zigarren, Zigaretten, Schokolade.

Frau Fischer: Eine Tafel[13] Schokolade, bitte.

Die Verkäuferin: Milchschokolade?

Frau Fischer: Ja, bitte. Was macht das?[14]

Die Verkäuferin: Sechzig Pfennig, bitte.

(*Frau Fischer bezahlt.[15]*)

Frau Fischer (*zu[16] Frau Schulz*): Nehmen Sie ein Stück[17] Schokolade?

Frau Schulz: Gern.[18] (*Sie nimmt[19] ein Stück.*) Danke schön. Die Schokolade ist gut.

Frau Fischer: Nehmen Sie noch[20] ein Stück.

Der Schaffner[21]: Die Fahrkarten[22] bitte.

Frau Schulz: Wann sind wir in Berlin?

Der Schaffner: Um elf Uhr fünfzehn.

Frau Fischer: Wieviel Uhr ist es jetzt?[23]

Herr Fischer: Zehn nach neun.[F]

---

[1] *in the train.*
[2] *from.*
[3] *to.*
[4] *other.*
[5] *is knitting.*
[6] *are looking.*
[7] *through.*
[8] *traveller.*
[9] *occupied.*
[10] der Verkäufer, -, *salesman.*
[11] die Zeitschrift, -en, *periodical.*
[12] die Verkäuferin,-nen, *saleslady.*
[13] die Tafel, -n, *tablet.*
[14] *How much?*
[15] *pays.*
[16] *to.*
[17] das Stück, -e, *piece.*
[18] *gladly.*
[19] *takes.*
[20] noch ein(e), *another.*
[21] der Schaffner, -, *guard.*
[22] die Fahrkarte, -n, *ticket.*
[23] *now.*

1.

Der Tisch	ist (nicht)	groß.	The table	is (not)	big.
Der Stuhl		klein.	The chair		small.
Der Platz		alt.	The seat		old.
ER		neu.	**IT**		new.
		gut.			good.
Die Tür		schlecht.	The door		bad.
Die Lampe		schön.	The lamp		beautiful.
Die Zeitung		häßlich.	The newspaper		ugly.
SIE			**IT**		
Das Buch			The book		
Das Fenster			The window		
Das Haus			The house		
Das Dorf			The village		
ES			**IT**		

2.

Die	Tische	sind (nicht)	groß.	The	tables	are (not)	big.
	Stühle		klein.		chairs		small.
	Plätze		alt.		seats		old.
	Türen		neu.		doors		new.
	Lampen		gut.		lamps		good.
	Zeitungen		schlecht.		newspapers		bad.
	Bücher		schön.		books		beautiful.
	Häuser		häßlich.		houses		ugly.
	Dörfer				villages		
	Fenster				windows		
SIE				**THEY**			

3.

Ist	der Tisch	(nicht)	groß?	Is	the table	(not)	big?
	er		klein?		it		small?
	die Lampe		alt?		the lamp		old?
	sie		neu?		it		new?
	das Buch		gut?		the book		good?
	es		schlecht?		it		bad?
			schön?				beautiful?
Sind	die Stühle		häßlich?	Are	the chairs		ugly?
	die Häuser				the houses		
	die Bücher				the books		
	sie				they		

4.

Ich nehme	ein Butterbrot.	I take	a slice of bread and butter.
Sie nehmen	ein Stück Schokolade.	You take	a piece of chocolate.
Er nimmt	eine Tasse Kaffee.	He takes	a cup of coffee.
Sie	ein Glas Bier.	She	a glass of beer.
Es	eine Flasche Wein.	It	a bottle of wine.
Nehmen Sie	noch ein Stück.	Take	another piece.
Nehmen Sie doch	noch eine Tasse.	Do take	another cup.

5. Es ist	ein[1]	Uhr.		It is	one	o'clock.
	zwei				two	
	drei				three	
	vier				four	
	fünf				five	
	sechs				six	
	sieben				seven	
	acht				eight	
	neun				nine	
	zehn				ten	
	elf				eleven	
	zwölf				twelve	

fünf nach zwölf.　　　　　　　　　 five past twelve.
(ein) Viertel eins.[2]　　　　　　 quarter past twelve.
halb eins.　　　　　　　　　　　　 half past twelve.
drei Viertel eins.[3]　　　　　　 quarter to one.
zehn vor eins.　　　　　　　　　　 ten to one.

[1] Ein Uhr *or* eins.　　[2] *or* (ein) Viertel nach zwölf.　　[3] *or* (ein) Viertel vor eins.

6. Wann	kommt der Zug an?	When	does the train arrive?
Um wieviel Uhr		At what time	
	beginnt das Konzert?		does the concert start?
	essen wir?		do we eat?
	fährt der Zug ab?		does the train leave?

Um sieben Uhr morgens.　　　　 At seven in the morning.
Um elf Uhr vormittags.　　　　　 At eleven a.m.
Um zwölf Uhr mittags.　　　　　 At twelve noon.
Um drei Uhr nachmittags.　　　 At three in the afternoon.
Um acht Uhr abends.　　　　　　 At eight in the evening.
Um zwölf Uhr nachts.　　　　　　 At twelve midnight.

7. Was	nimmt	der Vater?	What does	the father	take?
	ißt	die Mutter?		the mother	eat?
	trinkt	der Sohn?		the son	drink?
	liest	die Tochter?		the daughter	read?
	sieht	der ältere Herr?		the elderly gentleman	see?
	spricht	die junge Dame?		the young lady	speak?

8. Ist der Platz	frei?	Is the seat	vacant?
Sind die Plätze	besetzt?	Are the seats	occupied?
	bequem?		comfortable?
	unbequem?		uncomfortable?
	hoch?		high?
	niedrig?		low?

31

| 9. Ist | die Tür
das Fenster | offen?
zu?
breit? | | *Is* | *the door*
the window | *open?*
shut?
wide? |
| Sind | die Türen
die Fenster | schmal? | | *Are* | *the doors*
the windows | *narrow?* |

Explanations

1. *Er* (besides meaning he) = it, when replacing a masculine noun.

Sie (besides meaning she) = it, when replacing a feminine noun.

Es = it, when replacing a neuter noun.

2. The word *sie* can have three different meanings:

sie = she, when followed by the verb in singular, e.g. *sie ist*, she is.

sie = they, when followed by the verb in plural, e.g. *sie sind*, they are.

Sie = you, when spelt with a capital *S*.

3. *Die* = the, before any noun in plural.

4. Masculine nouns add *-e* in plural and modify *a*, *o*, *u*, e.g.

SINGULAR	der Hut, *hat*	PLURAL	die Hüte
	der Kamm, *comb*		die Kämme
	der Rock, *skirt*		die Röcke
	der Baum, *tree*		die Bäume

5. Feminine nouns add *-n* or *-en* in plural, e.g.

SINGULAR	die Blume, *flower*	PLURAL	die Blumen
	die Tür, *door*		die Türen
	die Frau, *woman*		die Frauen

6. Neuter nouns add *-e* in plural and do not modify, but many neuters of one syllable add *-er* and modify, e.g.

SINGULAR	das Gedicht, *poem*	PLURAL	die Gedichte
	das Jahr, *year*		die Jahre
	das Dach, *roof*		die Dächer
	das Buch, *book*		die Bücher
	das Dorf, *village*		die Dörfer
	das Haus, *house*		die Häuser

32

7. Masculine and neuter nouns ending in *-en*, *-el*, *-er* have no plural endings, but they modify *a*, *o*, *u*, e.g.

SINGULAR der Garten, *garden* PLURAL die Gärten
der Bruder, *brother* die Brüder
der Löffel, *spoon* die Löffel
das Messer, *knife* die Messer
das Fenster, *window* die Fenster
BUT die Gabel, *fork* die Gabeln

8. There are many exceptions to the above rules, e.g.

SINGULAR der Schuh, *shoe* PLURAL die Schuhe
der Tag, *day* die Tage
der Mann, *man* die Männer
der Wald, *forest* die Wälder
die Stadt, *town* die Städte
die Kuh, *cow* die Kühe
die Hand, *hand* die Hände
die Wand, *wall* die Wände
das Auge, *eye* die Augen
das Ohr, *ear* die Ohren
das Hemd, *shirt* die Hemden

C

Lektion Fünf

Dieser Kragen
ist zu eng.

Diese Hose
ist zu kurz.

Dieses Kleid
ist zu lang.

Der neue Hut
ist zu groß.

Die neuen Schuhe
sind zu klein.

IM ZUG (2)

Der Herr (*zu Frau Fischer*): Rauchen Sie?

Frau Fischer: Nein, danke, ich rauche nicht.

Der Herr (*zu Herrn Fischer*): Aber Sie rauchen, nicht wahr?

Herr Fischer (*nimmt eine Zigarette*): Sehr liebenswürdig.[1] Danke
schön! Das ist eine englische Zigarette, nicht wahr?

Der Herr: Nein, eine amerikanische.

Herr Fischer: Die amerikanischen Zigaretten sind sehr gut. Sind
Sie Amerikaner?

Der Herr: Ja, ich bin[F] Amerikaner.

Frau Fischer: Sie sprechen aber[2] gut deutsch.

[1] kind.   [2] but.

34

Der Herr: Oh, nur[3] ein wenig.[4] Ich verstehe[5] fast° alles,[7] aber ich spreche nicht sehr gut.

Frau Fischer (*zu Frau Schulz*): Fahren[8] Sie auch nach Berlin?

Frau Schulz: Ja, meine Eltern leben[9] in Berlin. Wir[10] leben in Hamburg.

Frau Fischer: Wir sind aus[11] Berlin. Wir waren[12] in Hamburg zu Besuch.[13] Meine ältere Tochter ist dort[14] verheiratet.[15]

Fritz: Schau[16] Mutti, die schwarze[17] Kuh!

Frau Fischer: Da[18] sind viele[19] Kühe.

Fritz: Die weißen Kühe geben[20] Milch, nicht wahr? Und die schwarzen, geben die[21] Kaffee?

---

[3] *only.*
[4] *little.*
[5] *understand.*
[6] *almost.*
[7] *everything.*
[8] *travel.*
[9] *live.*
[10] *we.*
[11] *from.*
[12] *were.*

[13] zu Besuch, *on a visit.*
[14] *there.*
[15] *married.*
[16] *look* (fam.).
[17] *black.*
[18] *there.*
[19] *many.*
[20] *give.*
[21] die, *they, is often used in the colloquial language instead of* sie.

FLUENCY PRACTICE

1. Der	Hut	ist	braun.	The	hat	is	brown.
Dieser	Rock		grau.	This	coat		grey.
Jener	Mantel		grün.	That	overcoat		green.
	Anzug		schwarz.		suit		black.

2. Die	Jacke	ist	weiß.	The	jacket	is	white.
Diese	Bluse		gelb.	This	blouse		yellow.
Jene	Krawatte		rot.	That	tie		red.
	Weste		blau.		waistcoat		blue.

3. Das	Kleid	ist	lang.	The	dress	is	long.
Dieses	Kostüm		kurz.	This	costume		short.
Jenes	Hemd		zu weit.	That	shirt		too wide.
			zu eng.				too tight.

4. Die	Jacken	sind	zu weit.	The	jackets	are	too wide.
Diese	Blusen		zu eng.	These	blouses		too tight.
Jene	Kleider		zu hell.	Those	dresses		too light.
	Kostüme		zu dunkel.		costumes		too dark.
	Hemden				shirts		
	Hosen				trousers		

35

Die	Hüte	sind	zu groß.		The	hats		are	too	big.
Diese	Röcke		zu klein.		These	coats			too	small.
Jene	Mäntel		zu lang.		Those	overcoats			too	long.
	Anzüge		zu kurz.			suits			too	short.

5.
Der große Tisch	ist	braun.		The big table	is	brown.
Die kleine Lampe		grün.		The small lamp		green.
Das neue Buch		rot.		The new book		red.
		blau.				blue.
		schwarz.				black.
Die großen Tische	sind	weiß.		The big tables	are	white.
Die kleinen Lampen		gelb.		The small lamps		yellow.
Die neuen Bücher		grau.		The new books		grey.

6.
ich	bin	groß.		I am		tall.
er	ist	klein.		He	is	short.
sie		dick.		She		stout.
es		dünn.		It		slim.
		jung.				young.
wir	sind	alt.		We	are	old.
Sie		müde.		You		tired.
sie				They		

7.
Sind	Sie	müde?		Are	you	tired?
	sie	krank?			they	ill?
		zufrieden?				pleased?
Ist	er	einverstanden?		Is	he	in agreement?
	sie				she	

8.
Wer ist	dieser Mann?	Who is	this man?
Wie heißt	diese Frau?	What is the name of	this woman?
	dieses Kind?		this child?
Wie heißt	dieser Ort?	What is the name of	this place?
	diese Stadt?		this town?
	dieses Dorf?		this village?

9.
Wer sind	diese	Männer?	Who are	these	men?
Wie heißen		Frauen?	What are the names of		women?
		Kinder?			children?

10.
Ich bin	Amerikaner.	I am	an American (man).
Sie sind	Amerikanerin.	You are	an American (woman).
	Engländer.		an Englishman.
	Engländerin.		an Englishwoman.
	Franzose.		a Frenchman.
	Französin.		a Frenchwoman.
	Italiener.		an Italian (man).
	Italienerin.		an Italian (woman).
	Schweizer.		a Swiss (man).
	Schweizerin.		a Swiss (woman).
	Österreicher.		an Austrian (man).
	Österreicherin.		an Austrian (woman).
	Deutscher.		a German (man).
	Deutsche.		a German (woman).

11.

Welcher	Hut / Anzug / Mantel	ist zu klein,	der braune oder der blaue? / dieser oder jener?
Welche	Jacke / Weste / Bluse	ist zu eng,	die gelbe oder die grüne? / diese oder jene?
Welches	Kleid / Kostüm / Hemd	ist zu lang,	das weiße oder das graue? / dieses oder jenes?
Welche	Hüte / Schuhe / Handschuhe	sind zu groß,	die schwarzen oder die braunen? / diese oder jene?

Which	hat / suit / coat	is too small,	the brown one or the blue one? / this one or that one?
Which	jacket / waistcoat / blouse	is too tight,	the yellow one or the green one? / this one or that one?
Which	dress / costume / shirt	is too long,	the white one or the grey one? / this one or that one?
Which	hats / shoes / gloves	are too big,	the black ones or the brown ones? / these or those?

12.

Welche Farbe hat	der neue Hut? / das neue Kleid? / die neue Bluse?
Welche Farbe haben	die neuen Schuhe? / die neuen Handschuhe? / die neuen Taschentücher?

What colour is	the new hat? / the new dress? / the new blouse?
What colour are	the new shoes? / the new gloves? / the new handkerchiefs?

1. dieser, *this*
   jener, *that* } before a masculine singular noun.
   welcher, *which*

2. dieses, *this*
   jenes, *that* } before a neuter singular noun.
   welches, *which*

3. diese { *this*, before a feminine singular noun.
          { *these*, before any noun in plural.

   jene { *that*, before a feminine singular noun.
         { *those*, before any noun in plural.

   welche { *which*, before a feminine singular noun.
           { *which*, before any noun in plural.

4. The adjective used in connection with *der*, *die*, *das* (or any of the words given above) ends in *-e* in singular and in *-en* in plural.

5. When the adjective is used predicatively (as in *er ist gut*, *sie sind zu klein*, etc.) it has no special ending.

6. Masculine nouns which in singular end in *-e* add *-n* in plural and they do not modify, e.g.

SINGULAR   der Knabe, *boy*[1]   PLURAL   die Knaben
           der Löwe, *lion*   die Löwen

To this group belong also some words which formerly ended in *-e*, e.g. *der Herr* in old German was *der Herre*, so the plural is still *die Herren*. Other such words are:

SINGULAR   der Soldat, *soldier*   PLURAL   die Soldaten
           der Bär, *bear*   die Bären
           der Student, *student*   die Studenten
           der Präsident, *president*   die Präsidenten
           der Prinz, *prince*   die Prinzen

[1] *or* der Junge, die Jungen.

Lektion Sechs

Sein Vater   Seine Mutter   Ihr Vater   Ihre Mutter

Seine Eltern   Ihre Eltern

Mein Vetter   Meine Kusine

Ihre Kinder

Das Baby   Der Junge   Das Mädel

IM ZUG (3)

A: *Der Schaffner.*[1]   B: *Ein Herr.*

A: Die Fahrkarten[2] bitte.

      (*Herr B. kann seine*[F] *Fahrkarte nicht finden*).

A: Wo ist Ihre[F] Fahrkarte?

B: Ich kann sie nicht finden.

A: Haben Sie eine oder haben Sie keine?[F]

B: Ich habe sie verloren.[3]

A: Wohin[4] fahren Sie?

B: Nach Berlin.

A: Acht Mark fünfzig, bitte.

B: Ich habe kein Geld.[5]

A: So! Sie haben keine[F] Fahrkarte und kein[F] Geld.

B: Ich habe mein Geld zu Hause. Hier habe ich nur zwei Mark.

A: Wie heißen[6] Sie?

B: Hans Berger.

A: Wo wohnen[7] Sie?

B: In Berlin.

A: Straße? Hausnummer?

B: Altgasse dreizehn.

A: Haben Sie Ausweispapiere?[8]

B: Hier ist mein Führerschein.[9]

A: Das ist ein alter Führerschein von 1950.

B: Hier ist mein Sparkassenbuch.[10]

A: Sie haben aber kein Geld auf der Sparkasse!

---

[1] der Schaffner, –, *guard.*
[2] die Fahrkarte, –n, *ticket.*
[3] *lost.*
[4] *where (to).*
[5] das Geld, *money.*
[6] Wie heißen Sie? *What is your name?*
   (*lit. how are you called?*)

[7] *live.*
[8] das Ausweispapier, –e, *identity paper.*
[9] der Führerschein, –e, *driving licence.*
[10] das Sparkassenbuch, –er, *savings bank book* (sparen, *to save*).

1.

Dies	ist	ein	schöner	Tisch.	This	is	a	beautiful	table.
Das		kein	guter	Hut.	That		not a	good	hat.
Hier		mein	neuer	Garten.	Here		my	new	garden.
Da		sein			There		his		
		ihr	schönes	Sofa.			her	beautiful	sofa.
		unser	gutes	Auto.			our	good	car.
		Ihr	neues	Haus.			your	new	house.
		ihr					their		

2.

Dies	ist	eine	schöne	Kommode.	This	is	a	beautiful	chest of drawers.
Das		keine	gute	Uhr.	That		not a	good	clock.
Hier		meine	neue	Villa.	Here		my	new	villa.
Da		seine			There		his		
		ihre					her		
		unsere					our		
		Ihre					your		
		ihre					their		

3.

Ist das nicht	ein schöner	Garten?	Isn't that a beautiful	garden?
		Baum?		tree?
		Ort?		place?
	eine schöne	Blume?		flower?
		Eiche?		oak?
		Buche?		beech?
	ein schönes	Haus?		house?
		Dorf?		village?
		Tier?		animal?

4.

Sind das nicht schöne	Bäume?	Aren't those beautiful	trees?
	Blumen?		flowers?
	Häuser?		houses?

5.

Die Herren	spielen Karten.	The gentlemen	are playing cards.
Die Damen	wohnen in Köln.	The ladies	live in Cologne.
Die Kinder	sitzen im Garten.	The children	are sitting in the garden.
	trinken Limonade.		drink lemonade.
Sie	essen Schokolade.	They	eat chocolate.
Wir	sind müde.	We	are tired.

Da ist	der Herr.		There is	the gentleman.
Da kommt	die Dame.		There comes	the lady.
Da sitzt	das Kind.		There sits	the child.

Kennen	Sie	ihn?	Do you	know	him?
Sehen		sie?		see	her?
		es?			it?

7.
Da sind	die Herren.		There are	the gentlemen.
Da kommen	die Damen.		There come	the ladies.
Da sitzen	die Kinder.		There sit	the children.

Kennen	Sie	sie?	Do you	know	them?
Sehen				see	

EXPLANATIONS

1. Adjectives preceded by *ein, kein, mein, sein, ihr, unser* take the following endings:

-*er* in connection with a masculine singular noun.

-*es* in connection with a neuter singular noun.

Adjectives preceded by *eine, keine, meine, seine, ihre, unsere* end in:

-*e* in connection with a feminine singular noun.

-*en* in connection with nouns in plural.

There is, of course, no plural of *ein* or *eine*, and the plural of *ein guter Apfel* is *gute Äpfel*, of *eine schöne Frau, schöne Frauen*, i.e. with the adjective ending in -*e*.

2. The verb in connection with *wir*, we, and *sie*, they, ends in -*en* (i.e. the same ending as with *Sie*, you).

3. *sie*, besides meaning 'she' and 'they', also stands for 'her' and 'them'.

4. Distinguish between the demonstrative adjectives *dieser, diese, dieses; jener, jene, jenes* (see Lesson V, Explanations 1–4), and the demonstrative pronouns *dies* and *das*, which are invariable:

dies ist, *this is*   das ist, *that is*

dies sind, *these are*   das sind, *those are*

42

Lektion Sieben

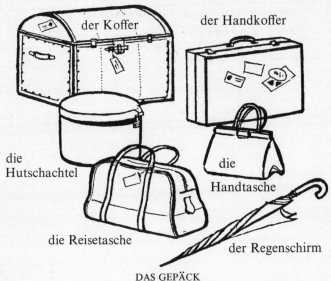

der Koffer

der Handkoffer

die Hutschachtel

die Handtasche

die Reisetasche

der Regenschirm

DAS GEPÄCK

DIE ANKUNFT[1]

Herr Fischer: Es ist zehn nach elf. In fünf Minuten sind wir da. Ich nehme[F] den großen[F] Koffer* und du kannst[2] die Reisetasche* nehmen.

Fritz: Kann ich nicht den kleinen Koffer nehmen?

Herr Fischer: Nein, er ist zu[3] schwer[4] für dich[5]. Ich nehme ihn.[F] Du kannst die Hutschachtel* nehmen.

Grete: Und ich nehme den Regenschirm.*

Frau Fischer: Sie müssen[6] uns in Berlin besuchen,[7] Frau Schulz. Wir ziehen[8] diese Woche[9] in eine neue Wohnung.[10]

Frau Schulz: Gern.

[1] *arrival.*
[2] *you* (fam.) *can* (*see Explanation* 6).
[3] *too.*
[4] *heavy.*
[5] *you* (fam.).
[6] *must.*
[7] *visit.*
[8] *move.*
[9] *week.*
[10] *flat.*

43

Herr Schulz: Sie müssen auch kommen, Herr Amerikaner. Unsere[1] neue Adresse ist Ahornallee 28, Berlin-Grunewald. Schreiben Sie sie auf.[2] Haben Sie keinen[F] Bleistift? Nehmen Sie meinen![F]

[1] our.   [2] down.

FLUENCY PRACTICE

1. ich habe	einen Bleistift.		*I*	*have*	*a pencil.*
du hast	eine Füllfeder.		*You* (fam.)		*a fountain pen.*
Sie | haben	ein Taschenmesser.		*You*		*a pocket knife.*
wir	Bleistifte.		*We*		*pencils.*
sie	Federn.		*They*		*pens.*
	Bücher.				*books.*
er | hat			*He*	*has*	
sie			*She*		
es			*It*		

2. Wer hat	einen	Teller?	*Who has*	*a*		*plate?*
	keinen	Löffel?		*no*		*spoon?*
Haben Sie	meinen	Regenschirm?	*Have you*	*my*		*umbrella?*
Hast du	seinen	Regenmantel?		*his*		*raincoat?*
	deinen	Wintermantel?		*your* (fam.)		*winter coat?*
	Ihren			*your* (polite)		
	ihren			*her* (or *their*)		
	unseren			*our*		
	eine	Tasse?		*a*		*cup?*
	keine	Gabel?		*no*		*fork?*
	meine	Flasche Milch?		*my*		*bottle of milk?*
	seine	Schachtel Streichhölzer?		*his*		*box of*
	deine			*your* (fam.)		*matches?*
	Ihre	Füllfeder?		*your*		*fountain pen?*
	ihre			*her* (or *their*)		
	unsere			*our*		
	ein	Taschentuch?		*a*		*handkerchief?*
	kein	Wörterbuch?		*no*		*dictionary?*
	mein	Briefpapier?		*my*		*note-paper?*
	sein	Taschenmesser?		*his*		*penknife?*
	dein	Handtuch?		*your* (fam.)		*towel?*
	Ihr			*your* (polite)		
	ihr			*her* (or *their*)		
	unser			*our*		

3. Wer hat	meine	Handschuhe?	*Who has*	*my*		*gloves?*
	deine	Taschentücher?		*your* (fam.)		*handkerchiefs?*
Hast du	Ihre	Briefumschläge?	*Have you*	*your* (pol.)		*envelopes?*
Heben Sie	seine	Streichhölzer?		*his*		*matches?*
	ihre	Kaffeetassen?		*her*		*coffee cups?*
	unsere			*our*		

44

4.

Nehmen Sie	einen	Löffel.	*Take*	*a*	*spoon.*
Nimm	den			*the*	
Geben Sie mir	eine	Gabel.	*Give me*	*a*	*fork.*
Gib mir	die			*the*	
Vergessen Sie nicht					
Vergiß nicht	ein	Messer.	*Don't forget*	*a*	*knife.*
	das			*the*	
	die	Löffel.		*the*	*spoons.*
		Gabeln.			*forks.*
		Messer.			*knives.*

5.

Wo haben Sie	den	Regenschirm?	*Where have you*	*the*	*umbrella?*
	Ihren			*your*	
	ihn?			*it?*	
	die	Tasche?		*the*	*bag?*
	Ihre			*your*	
	sie?			*it?*	
	das	Handgepäck?		*the*	*hand luggage?*
	Ihr			*your*	
	es?			*it?*	
	die	Sachen?		*the*	*things?*
	Ihre			*your*	
	sie?			*them?*	

6.

ich nehme		diesen Koffer.	*I take*		*this suitcase.*
du nimmst		ihn.	*You take*		*it.*
		diese Tasche.			*this bag.*
er	nimmt	sie.	*He*	*takes*	*it.*
sie		dieses Kissen.	*She*		*this cushion.*
		es.			*it.*
wir	nehmen	diese	Koffer.	*We*	*take*	*these*	*suitcases.*
Sie			Taschen.	*You*			*bags.*
sie			Kissen.	*They*			*cushions.*
		sie.			*them.*

7.

ich habe	einen	großen	Hund.	*I have*	*a*	*large*	*dog.*
du hast		kleinen	Garten.	*You have*		*small*	*garden.*
		schönen	Schrank.			*nice*	*cupboard.*
		guten				*good*	
er	hat	eine	große	Katze.	*He*	*has*	*a*	*large*	*cat.*
sie			kleine	Villa.	*She*			*small*	*villa.*
es			schöne	Stube.	*It*			*nice*	*room.*
			gute					*good*	
wir	haben	ein	großes	Auto.	*We*	*have*	*a*	*large*	*car.*
Sie			kleines	Haus.	*You*			*small*	*house.*
sie			schönes	Bett.	*They*			*nice*	*bed.*
			gutes					*good*	
		große	Briefumschläge.			*large*	*envelopes.*
		kleine	Taschentücher.			*small*	*handkerchiefs.*
		schöne	Notizbücher.			*nice*	*note-books.*
		gute				*good*	

EXPLANATIONS

1. *Den, einen, meinen, seinen*, etc. are used only with masculine singular nouns when they are the direct object in a sentence. In the sentence *der Hut ist blau, der Hut* is the subject of the sentence and is said to be in the Nominative case, whereas in *ich nehme den blauen Hut, Hut* is the direct object and is in the Accusative case.

2. Adjectives used in connection with a masculine noun in the Accusative end in *-en*.

3. *Ihn*, besides meaning 'him', also stands for 'it', replacing a masculine noun in the Accusative case.

Similarly, *sie*, besides meaning 'her', also stands for 'it', replacing a feminine noun in the Accusative case. When replacing nouns in plural *sie* stands for both 'they' and 'them'.

Thus a distinction between Nominative and Accusative is made only with masculines in the singular, so that the word *sie* is used for 'she' and 'her', 'they' and 'them'.

4. A child, a near relative or an intimate friend are addressed as *du*. The verb used in connection with *du* ends in *-st*: *du bist*, you are; *du hast*, you have; *kommst du?* are you coming? When there is a change of vowel in the third person singular (see Lesson III, Explanation 3), this also applies to the *du* form of the verb (the second person singular): *du gibst*, you give, *du liest*, you read, *du nimmst*, you take, etc. The corresponding imperatives are *komm! gib! lies! nimm!*

Your in the familiar form is *dein(e): dein Vater, deine Mutter, deine Eltern*.

5. *Ich liebe dich*, I love you. *Liebst du mich?* Do you love me? *Mich* and *dich* are the accusatives of *ich* and *du*.

6. *Welchen Koffer nehmen Sie, diesen oder jenen?* Which suitcase are you taking, this one or that one?

Note that *welcher, dieser, jener* change to *welchen, diesen, jenen* in the Accusative case.

Lektion Acht

der Kleiderschrank

die Kommode

das Bett

der Sessel

DAS ZIMMER

DAS HOTEL

(*Georg Heimann, der Amerikaner, kommt in die Eingangshalle[1] eines Hotels.*)

Georg: Haben Sie ein Zimmer* frei?

Empfangsherr[2]: Für Sie allein?[3]

Georg: Ja, für eine Person.

Empfangsherr: Wir haben ein schönes, großes Zimmer mit Bad[4] im ersten[5] Stock.[6] Möchten[7] Sie es sehen?

Georg: Ja, bitte. (*Sie nehmen den Fahrstuhl.[8]*)

Empfangsherr: Hier ist das Zimmer. Sie haben einen großen Kleiderschrank,* einen Schreibtisch[9] und einen Sessel.* Und hier ist das Bett.* Es ist sehr bequem.[10]

---

[1] *entrance hall.*
[2] *receptionist.*
[3] *alone; by yourself.*
[4] das Bad, ⁻er, *bath.*
[5] *first.*

[6] *short for* das Stockwerk, –e, *floor.*
[7] *would you like.*
[8] der Fahrstuhl, –stühle, *lift.*
[9] der Schreibtisch, –e, *writing desk.*
[10] *comfortable.*

47

Georg: Wo ist das Badezimmer?

Empfangsherr: Hier nebenan.[1]

Georg: Was kostet das Zimmer?

Empfangsherr: Acht Mark fünfzig pro Tag.

Georg: Mit Frühstück?[2]

Empfangsherr: Nein, das Frühstück ist nicht einbegriffen.[3]

Georg: Das ist zu[4] teuer.[5] Haben Sie kein[6] billigeres[7] Zimmer?

Empfangsherr: Wir haben ein kleineres Zimmer im vierten[8] Stock.

Georg: Ist es viel kleiner?

Empfangsherr: Es ist natürlich nicht so groß wie dieses Zimmer. Es hat keinen Schreibtisch und der Kleiderschrank ist nicht so groß wie[F] dieser. Es ist natürlich billiger. Nur[9] sechs Mark.

Georg: Das ist viel besser.

Empfangsherr: Möchten Sie es sehen?

Georg: Gern.[10]

[1] *adjoining.*
[2] das Frühstück, –e, *breakfast.*
[3] *included.*
[4] *too.*
[5] *expensive.*
[6] *no.*
[7] *cheaper.*
[8] *fourth.*
[9] *only.*
[10] *gladly.*

FLUENCY PRACTICE

1.
ich esse	gern	Schokolade.	*I*	*like*	*eating*	*chocolate.*
du	ißt	Kalbfleisch.	*You*			*veal.*
		Schweinefleisch.				*pork.*
er		Rindfleisch.	*He*	*likes*		*beef.*
sie		Hammelfleisch.	*She*			*mutton.*
		Erdbeeren.				*strawberries.*
wir	essen		*We*	*like*		
Sie			*You*			
sie			*They*			

ich trinke	gern	Tee.	*I*	*like*	*drinking*	*tea.*
du trinkst		Kaffee.	*You*			*coffee.*
		Kakao.				*cocoa.*
er	trinkt	Milch.	*He*	*likes*		*milk.*
sie		Limonade.	*She*			*lemonade.*
		Weißwein.				*white wine.*
wir	trinken	Rotwein.	*We*	*like*		*red wine.*
Sie		helles Bier.	*You*			*light beer.*
sie		dunkles Bier.	*They*			*dark beer.*

2.

German:

	ist (nicht) so		wie	
Der Tisch		groß		der Sessel.
Die Tür		klein		die Kommode.
Das Fenster		lang		das Sofa.
Der Kleiderschrank		breit		der Küchenschrank.
Der Bücherschrank		hoch		das Büffet.
		niedrig		
		gut		

English:

	is (not) as		as the	
The table		big		armchair.
The door		small		chest of drawers.
The window		long		sofa.
The wardrobe		wide		kitchen cupboard.
The bookcase		high		sideboard.
		low		
		good		

3.

German:

	ist (nicht)		als	
Der Schreibtisch		größer		die Kommode.
Das Küchenfenster		kleiner		der Küchenschrank.
Die Badezimmertür		länger		das Büffet.
Der Kleiderschrank		breiter		
		höher		
		niedriger		
		besser		

English:

	is (not)		than	
The desk		bigger		the chest of drawers.
The kitchen window		smaller		the kitchen cupboard.
The bathroom door		longer		the sideboard.
The wardrobe		wider		
		higher		
		lower		
		better		

4.

German:

	(nicht) so	viel		wie	
ich habe		viel	Geld		Sie.
er hat			Brot		du.
sie			Käse		er.
					sie.
					wir.

	(nicht) so	viele			
wir haben		viele	Bücher		sie.
Sie			Hüte		mein Vater.
sie			Schuhe		meine Mutter.

English:

	(not) as	much		as	
I have		much	money		you.
He has			bread		he.
She			cheese		she.
					we.

	(not) as	many			
We have		many	books		they.
You			hats		my father.
They			shoes		my mother.

5.

German:

	(nicht) mehr		als	
ich habe		Geld		er.
er hat		Fleisch		sie.
sie		Schokolade		du.
wir haben		Äpfel		Sie.
Sie		Birnen		wir.
sie		Bananen		Karl.
				Grete.

English:

	(not) more		than	
I have		money		he.
He has		meat		she.
She		chocolate		you.
We have		apples		we.
You		pears		Karl.
They		bananas		Grete.

1. größer, *taller*
   älter, *older*
   kürzer, *shorter*
   intelligenter, *more intelligent*
   besser, *better*

The comparative of adjectives is formed by adding *-er*, whilst modifying *a, o, u*. The comparative of *gut*, as in English, is irregular.

2. der | größte | *the* | *tallest*
   die | längste | | *longest*
   das | kürzeste | | *shortest*
   | intelligenteste | | *most intelligent*
   | beste | | *best*

The superlative of adjectives is formed by adding *-ste*, whilst modifying *a, o, u*. Words ending in *t* or *z* add *-este*, to make them easier to pronounce.

3. gern, *gladly*.
   ich tanze gern, *I like dancing*.
   ich esse gern Schokolade, *I like eating chocolate*.

To say that you like doing something is expressed by saying that you do it gladly.

Lektion Neun

Der Kragen liegt
auf der Kommode.

Der Mantel hängt
an der Tür.

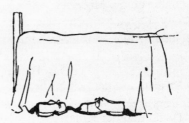

Das Hemd hängt
über dem Stuhl.

Die Schuhe stehen
unter dem Bett.

Der Schlips liegt
auf dem Fußboden vor dem Stuhl.

DAS FRÜHSTÜCK[1]

Georg (*telephoniert*): Bringen[F] Sie mir bitte mein Frühstück.[1]
Zimmer Nummer zwölf.

Der Zimmerkellner[2]: Tee, Kaffee oder Kakao?

Georg: Kaffee, bitte.

[1] das Frühstück, -e, *breakfast*.   [2] der Zimmerkellner, -, *room waiter*.

Zimmerkellner: Möchten[1] Sie Eier?[2] Setzei,[3] Rührei,[4] gekochte[5] Eier?

Georg: Ein gekochtes Ei, bitte.

Zimmerkellner: Weich[6] oder hart?

Georg: Weich gekocht, bitte.

Kellner: Ich bringe es Ihnen[F] in fünf Minuten.

(*Georg geht ins[F] Badezimmer. In fünf Minuten klopft[7] der Zimmerkellner an seine Tür.*)

Georg: Wer ist da?

Kellner: Der Zimmerkellner. Ich bringe Ihnen das Frühstück.

Georg: Kommen Sie herein! Ich bin im[E] Badezimmer.

Kellner: Guten Morgen!

Georg: Guten Morgen! Was gibt[8] es zum Frühstück?

Kellner: Kaffee, Brötchen,[9] Butter, Honig,[10] ein gekochtes Ei.

Georg: Geben Sie mir bitte mein Hemd,* meinen Kragen* und meinen Schlips.[11] Das Hemd hängt über* dem Stuhl. Der Kragen und der Schlips liegen auf* der Kommode.[12]

Kellner (*gibt[F] ihm[F] das Hemd und den Kragen*): Hier sind das Hemd und der Kragen. Ich kann den Schlips nicht finden.

Georg: Liegt er nicht auf der Kommode?

Kellner: Nein, da liegt er nicht.

Georg: Hängt er nicht über dem Stuhl?

Kellner: Nein, da hängt er auch nicht.—Da liegt er. Auf dem Fußboden[13] vor* dem Stuhl.

Georg (*kommt aus dem Badezimmer*): Wo ist der Zucker?

Kellner: Entschuldigen[14] Sie, ich habe ihn vergessen.[15] Ich bringe ihn gleich.[16]

---

[1] ich möchte, *I should like.*
[2] das Ei, –er, *egg.*
[3] *fried egg*
[4] *scrambled eggs.*
[5] *boiled.*
[6] *soft.*
[7] klopfen, *to knock.*
[8] Was gibt es? *What is there?*

[9] das Brötchen, –, *roll.*
[10] der Honig, *honey.*
[11] der Schlips, –e, *tie.*
[12] die Kommode, *chest of drawers.*
[13] der Fußboden, -ö-, *floor.*
[14] *excuse.*
[15] *forgotten.*
[16] *at once.*

1.

This watch	belongs to	the teacher (m.).
This ring		the teacher (f.).
This brooch		
This		me.
That		us.
It (m.)		you.
It (f.)		
It (n.)		

Diese Uhr	gehört	dem Lehrer.
Dieser Ring		ihm.
Diese Brosche		der Lehrerin.
Dies		ihr.
Das		mir.
Er		uns.
Sie		Ihnen.
Es		

2.

I am	going to	my	father.
	coming from	his	brother.
	staying with	her	uncle.
He	is	my	mother.
She		his	sister.
		her	aunt.
You	are	my	parents.
We		our	brothers and sisters.
They		his	friends (m.).
		her	friends (f.).

ich	gehe zu	meinem	Vater.
	komme von	seinem	Bruder.
	bleibe bei	ihrem	Onkel.
er	geht zu	meiner	Mutter.
sie	kommt von	seiner	Schwester.
	bleibt bei	ihrer	Tante.
Sie	gehen zu	meinen	Eltern.
wir	kommen von	unseren	Geschwistern.
sie	bleiben bei	seinen	Freunden.
		ihren	Freundinnen.

3.

I	write	to my brother.
	reply	to my sister.
	give this	to my friends (m.).
	bring something	to his friend (m.).
	send the parcel	to his friend (f.).
		to his friends (m.).
He	gives this	to her friend (m.).
She	brings that	to her friend (f.).
	sends it (n.).	to her friends (m.).
		to her friends (f.).

ich	schreibe	meinem Bruder.
	antworte	meiner Schwester.
	gebe dies	meinen Freunden.
	bringe etwas	seinem Freund.
	sende das Paket	seiner Freundin.
		seinen Freunden.
er	gibt dies	ihrem Freund.
sie	bringt das	ihrer Freundin.
	sendet es	ihren Freunden.
		ihren Freundinnen.

4.

Does	this	belong to	you?
	that		your father?
	this trunk		your mother?
	this bag		your parents?
	this book		the parents?
			the children?
Do	these things		your children?
	they		them?

4. Gehört	dies		Ihnen?
	das		Ihrem Vater?
	dieser Koffer		Ihrer Mutter?
	diese Tasche		den Eltern?
	dieses Buch		Ihren Eltern?
			den Kindern?
Gehören	diese Sachen		Ihren Kindern?
	sie		ihnen?

5.

Give	me		your pencil.
Bring	my friend (m.)		your fountain pen.
Show	him		your dictionary.
Send	my friend (f.)		your coloured pencils.
Lend	her		
	my friends (m.)		
	them		

	it	to	me.
			my friend (m.).
			him.
			my friend (f.).
			her.
	them		my friends (m.).
			them.

5. Geben Sie	mir		Ihren Bleistift!
Bringen Sie	meinem Freund		Ihre Füllfeder!
Zeigen Sie	ihm		Ihr Wörterbuch!
Senden Sie	meiner Freundin		Ihre Buntstifte!
Leihen Sie	ihr		
	meinen Freunden		
	ihnen		

	ihn	mir.
	sie	meinem Freund.
	es	ihm.
		meiner Freundin.
	sie	ihr.
		meinen Freunden.
		ihnen.

6.

I give		you	the money.
He	gives	you (fam.)	twenty marks.
She		the gentleman	thirty pfennig.
		the lady	15.40 marks.
We	give	the young lady	not a penny.
You		the children	
They			

6. ich gebe		Ihnen	das Geld.
er	gibt	dir	zwanzig Mark.
sie		dem Herrn	dreißig Pfennig.
		der Dame	fünfzehn Mark vierzig.
wir	geben	dem Fräulein	nicht einen Pfennig.
Sie		den Kindern	
sie			

7. WOHIN GEHEN SIE?

Ich gehe | zum[1] Friseur.
| zum Schneider.
| zu meinem Onkel.
| zu meiner Tante.
| zur[2] Schneiderin.

WHERE ARE YOU GOING?

I am going | to the hairdresser's (m.).
| to the tailor's.
| to my uncle's.
| to my aunt's.
| to the dressmaker's.

8. WO IST GEORG?

Er ist beim[3] Friseur.
Er ist beim Schneider.
Er ist bei seinem Onkel.

WHERE IS GEORGE?

He is at the hairdresser's (m.).
He is at the tailor's.
He is at his uncle's.

9. WO IST LUISE?

Sie ist bei der Friseuse.
Sie ist bei der Schneiderin.
Sie ist bei ihrer Tante.

WHERE IS LOUISE?

She is at the hairdresser's (f.).
She is at the dressmaker's.
She is at her aunt's.

10. WOHER KOMMEN SIE?

Ich komme vom[4] Friseur.
Ich komme von der Friseuse.
Ich komme vom Schneider.
Ich komme von der Schneiderin.
Ich komme von meinem Onkel.
Ich komme von meiner Tante.
Ich komme von meinen Eltern.

WHERE ARE YOU COMING FROM?

I am coming from the hairdresser's (m.).
I am coming from the hairdresser's (f.).
I am coming from the tailor's.
I am coming from the dressmaker's.
I am coming from my uncle's.
I am coming from my aunt's.
I am coming from my parents'.

[1] zum = zu dem.   [2] zur = zu der.   [3] beim = bei dem.   [4] vom = von dem.

55

SUBJECT	DIRECT OBJECT	INDIRECT OBJECT
(*in the Nominative*)	(*in the Accusative*)	(*in the Dative*)
ich, *I*	mich, *me*	mir, *to me*
er, *he, it*	ihn, *him, it*	ihm, *to him*
sie, *she, it*	sie, *her, it*	ihr, *to her*
es, *it*	es, *it*	ihm, *to it*
sie, *they*	sie, *them*	ihnen, *to them*
Sie, *you*	Sie, *you*	Ihnen, *to you*
du, *you* (fam.)	dich, *you* (fam.)	dir, *to you* (fam.)
wir, *we*	uns, *us*	uns, *to us*

2. dem, *to the*
diesem, *to this*
jenem, *to that*
einem, *to a*
meinem, *to my*
seinem *to his, to its*
ihrem, *to her*
Ihrem, *to your*

} with masculine and neuter nouns which are the indirect object of a sentence in the singular, e.g. in the sentence *Ich gebe meinem Vater ein Buch*, what I actually give (*ein Buch*) is the direct object, whereas *meinem Vater* is the indirect object. The indirect object is said to be in the Dative case.

der, *to the*
dieser, *to this*
jener, *to that*
einer, *to a*
meiner, *to my*
seiner, *to his*
ihrer, *to her, to their*
Ihrer, *to your*

} with feminine nouns in the singular in the Dative case.

den, *to the*
diesen, *to these*
jenen, *to those*
meinen, *to my*
ihren, *to her, to their*
Ihren, *to your*

} with nouns in plural in the Dative case. In the Dative case plural, -*n* is added to the noun, e.g. *den Kindern* to the children.

3. The prepositions *zu*, to; *von*, from; *bei*, at; *nach*,[1] after, are followed by the Dative case.

4. The prepositions *auf*, on; *über*, over; *unter*, under; *vor*, before; *hinter*, behind; *neben*, beside; *an*, at; *zwischen*, between, are also used with the Dative, but in certain cases, explained in Lesson XII, they require the Accusative.

5. Learn to distinguish between the Dative case and the preposition *zu*. In 'She brings flowers to her teacher' *to* is merely an indication of the Dative case, which can be omitted in English by saying 'She brings her teacher flowers'. This would be in German *Sie bringt ihrer Lehrerin Blumen*, i.e. the word 'to' is not translated at all and 'to her teacher' is expressed by the Dative case.

In 'We are going to my aunt's,' *Wir gehen zu meiner Tante*, 'to' cannot be omitted in English, nor *zu* in German.

6. Some prepositions may be contracted with the definite article: *ins = in das; im = in dem; zum = zu dem; zur = zu der; vom = von dem; beim = bei dem; am = an dem; aufs = auf das*.

7. *Jeder Mann, jede Frau und jedes Kind.* Each man, each woman, each child.

Geben Sie jedem Herrn eine Zigarre, jeder Dame eine Rose und jedem Kind eine Tafel Schokolade. Give each man a cigar, each lady a rose and each child a bar of chocolate.

Jeder, jede, jedes, each, every, are declined like *der, die, das*.

---

[1] Nach *also means* to *when indicating direction to a place, e.g.* nach Hause gehen, *to go home.*

Lektion Zehn

das Pferd
(der Kopf des Pferdes)

der Hund
(die Beine des Hundes)

die Katze
(der Schwanz der Katze)

IM SCHREIBWARENGESCHÄFT[1]

A: *Georg.* B: *der Portier.* C: *Erste Kundin.*[2] D: *Zweite Kundin.*
    E: *Erster Verkäufer.*[3] F: *Zweiter Verkäufer.*

A (*im Vestibül des Hotels zum Portier*): Ist hier ein Schreibwaren-
    geschäft in der Nähe?[4]

B: Drei Minuten von hier. Gehen Sie die Straße nach links[5]
    hinauf[6] bis[7] zur Post.[8] Gegenüber[9] der Post ist ein Schreib-
    warengeschäft.

[1] das Schreibwarengeschäft, –e,
    stationery shop.
[2] der Kunde, –n, die Kundin, –nen,
    customer.
[3] der Verkäufer, –, *salesman.*
[4] die Nähe, *neighbourhood.*

[5] *left.*
[6] *up.*
[7] bis zu, *up to, until.*
[8] die Post, *post office* (*short for* das
    Postamt, -ämter).
[9] *opposite.*

A: Ich danke Ihnen!

(*Georg folgt den Anweisungen[1] des Portiers, geht die Straße nach links hinauf bis zur Post, überquert[2] die Straße und geht ins Schreibwarengeschäft. Im Geschäft[3] sind mehrere[4] Kunden.*)

C: Die Farbe[5] des Schreibpapiers gefällt[F] mir nicht. Haben Sie kein dunkleres?[6]

D: Die Größe dieses Kastens[7] gefällt mir nicht. Haben Sie keinen kleineren?

C: Die Qualität dieser Umschläge[8] gefällt mir nicht. Haben Sie keine besseren?

D: Was kostet dieser Kasten?

E: Vier Mark zwanzig.

D: Haben Sie keinen billigeren?[9]

E: Dieser ist billiger.

D: Aber er gefällt mir nicht. Die anderen[10] sind zu teuer. Ich werde[11] woanders[12] versuchen.[13] Auf Wiedersehen!

E: Guten Morgen!

A: Geben Sie mir bitte einen Schreibblock und zwanzig Umschläge.

F: Weiße oder farbige?

A: Weiße, bitte! (*Der Verkäufer zeigt[14] ihm verschiedene.[15]*) Ja, die sind recht.[16] Und diesen Schreibblock. Was macht das?

F: Achtzig Pfennig der Schreibblock und vierzig Pfennig die Umschläge. (*Er flüstert[17] dem andern Verkäufer ins Ohr.*) Solche[18] Kunden gefallen mir.

---

[1] die Anweisung, –en, *indication, direction.*
[2] *crosses.*
[3] das Geschäft, –e, *business; shop.*
[4] *several.*
[5] die Farbe, –n, *colour.*
[6] dunkel, *dark.*
[7] der Kasten, –, *box, case.*
[8] der Umschlag, ⸚e, *envelope.*
[9] billig, *cheap.*
[10] *others.*
[11] *shall.*
[12] *somewhere else.*
[13] *try.*
[14] *shows.*
[15] *various.*
[16] *right.*
[17] *whispers.*
[18] *such.*

1.

Der Hut	des Lehrers der Lehrerin des Kindes meines Bruders meiner Schwester	ist	blau. braun. schwarz. zu groß. zu klein.
The teacher's (m.) The teacher's (f.) The child's My brother's My sister's		hat is	blue. brown. black. too big. too small.

2.

Die Farbe	des Hutes des Kleides des Mantels der Bluse der Krawatte der Schuhe	gefällt	mir ihm ihr ihnen uns	(nicht).
I (don't) He (doesn't) She „ They (don't) We „	like the colour of the	hat. dress. coat. blouse. tie. shoes.		

3.

Die Schuhe Die Krawatten Die Handschuhe Die Bücher Die Freunde Die Freundinnen	meines Bruders meiner Schwester seines Freundes seiner Freundin unseres Lehrers unserer Lehrerin ihrer Kinder	gefallen	mir ihm ihr ihnen uns	(nicht).
I (don't) He (doesn't) She „ They (don't) We „	like	the shoes the ties the gloves the books the friends (m.) the friends (f.)	of	my brother. my sister. his friend (m.). his friend (f.). our teacher (m.). our teacher (f.) her (or their) children.

4.

Wegen Trotz Während	des schlechten Wetters des starken Regens der Feiertage	kann er (nicht) kommen.
Because of In spite of During	the bad weather the heavy rain the holidays	he can(not) come.

5.

Mit	dem blauen Bleistift der schlechten Feder seinen neuen Bleistiften	kann ich können Sie können wir	nicht schreiben.

With	the blue pencil the bad pen his new pencils	I you we	cannot write.

6.

Mit	der Feder dem Bleistift	schreibe ich.

Aus	der Tasse dem Glas	trinke ich.

Von	meinem Onkel meiner Tante	borge ich.

With	the pen the pencil	I write.

Out of	the cup the glass.	I drink.

From	my uncle my aunt	I borrow.

7. Beim Bäcker kaufen wir Brot.
Bei der Bank wechseln wir unser ausländisches Geld.
Zum Schneider gehe ich, wenn ich einen neuen Anzug brauche.
Zur Schneiderin gehe ich, wenn ich ein neues Kleid brauche.
Vor dem Frühstück lese ich die Zeitung.
Vor der deutschen Stunde trinke ich eine Tasse Kaffee.
Nach dem Abendessen gehen wir spazieren.
Nach der Arbeit ruhen wir.
Seit wann sind Sie hier?
Wir sind seit einer halben Stunde hier.

At the baker's we buy bread.
At the bank we change our foreign money.
I go to the tailor when I need a new suit.
I go to the dressmaker when I need a new dress.
Before breakfast I read the newspaper.
Before the German lesson I drink a cup of coffee.
After the evening meal we go for a walk.
After work we rest.
How long[1] have you been here?
We have been here for half an hour.

61

---

[1] lit. 'since when', followed by the Present tense in German.

1. des, *of the*
   eines, *of a*
   meines, *of my*
   seines, *of his, of its*
   ihres, *of her*
   dieses, *of this*
   jenes, *of that*

   before masculine and neuter nouns in singular, when they are in the Genitive (or Possessive) case.
   Note that the noun takes the ending -s (-es in words of one syllable), e.g. *meines Vaters*, my father's; *des Pferdes*, the horse's.

   der, *of the*
   einer, *of a*
   meiner, *of my*
   seiner, *of his, of its*
   ihrer, *of her*
   dieser, *of this, of these*
   jener, *of that, of those*

   before feminine nouns in singular, or any noun in plural, when they are in the Genetive (or Possessive) case. There are no endings added to the noun, which retains its normal plural form, e.g. *der Kinder*.

Note that 'my wife's handbag' is expressed as 'the handbag of my wife' (*die Handtasche meiner Frau*). Only with proper names can a Genitive in -s be used as in English, e.g. *Walters Schuhe, Gretes Mutter*.

2. *gefallen*, to please. To say that you like something is expressed by saying that it pleases you, e.g. *Diese Farbe gefällt mir*, I like this colour.

The way to say that you like doing something has been explained in Lesson VIII, Explanation 3.

3. The following prepositions are followed by the noun (or pronoun) in the Genitive case: *wegen*, because of; *trotz*, in spite of; *während*, during.

4. The prepositions *mit*, with; *aus*, out of; *seit*, since, require the Dative case. See also Lesson IX, Explanation 3.

5. Adjectives used in connection with nouns in either the Dative or the Genitive case end in -*en*.

Lektion Elf

die Erdbeere

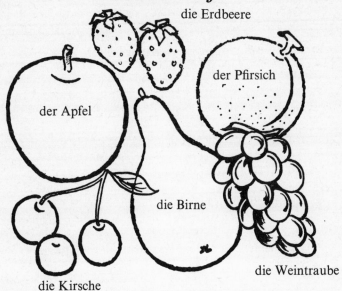

der Pfirsich

der Apfel

die Birne

die Kirsche

die Weintraube

IM OBSTGESCHÄFT[1]

K: *die Kundin.*   V: *der Verkäufer.*

K: Was kosten die Äpfel?*

V: Sechzig[2] Pfennig das Pfund.

K: Haben Sie keine billigeren?

V: Wir haben auch eine billigere Sorte zu vierzig Pfennig. Es sind aber Kochäpfel.[3]

K: Ich nehme drei Pfund zu vierzig. Haben Sie süße[4] Apfelsinen?[5]

V: Die Jaffa-Apfelsinen sind die süßesten.

K: Was kosten sie?

V: Eine Mark achtzig das Dutzend.[6]

---

[1] das Obstgeschäft, –e. *fruit shop.*
[2] *sixty.*
[3] *cooking apples.*

[4] *sweet.*
[5] die Apfelsine, -n, *orange.*
[6] *dozen.*

K: Geben Sie mir ein halbes[1] Dutzend. Sind die Melonen reif?[2]

V: Hier ist eine schöne, reife.

K: Haben Sie keine größeren?

V: Dies ist die größte. Sie ist aber noch nicht[3] ganz[4] reif.

K (*nimmt die kleinere*): Was kostet diese?

V: Eine Mark zwanzig das Pfund.

K: Wieviel wiegt[5] sie?

V (*legt die Melone auf die Waage*[6]): Sie wiegt genau[7] dreieinhalb Pfund.

K: Ich nehme sie. Was macht das zusammen?[8]

V: 1,20 M die Äpfel, 90 Pfennig die Apfelsinen und 4,20 M die Melone. Das macht zusammen 6,30 M.

K: Ich habe leider[9] kein Kleingeld. Können Sie mir bitte auf hundert Mark herausgeben?[10]

V: Aber gewiß,[11] gnädige Frau.[12] (*Er nimmt den Hundertmark-schein*[13] *und gibt der Kundin 93,70 M heraus.*) Vier Zwanzig-markscheine, ein Zehnmarkschein, drei Mark und siebzig Pfennig.

[1] *half.*
[2] *ripe.*
[3] noch nicht, *not yet.*
[4] *quite; entirely.*
[5] *weighs.*
[6] die Waage, –n, *scales; weighing machine.*
[7] *exactly.*
[8] *together.*
[9] *unfortunately.*
[10] *to give change.*
[11] *certainly.*
[12] gnädige Frau, *Madam* (*lit., gracious woman*).
[13] der Schein, –e, *note.*

FLUENCY PRACTICE

1. Essen Sie gern	Fleisch? Fisch? Obst? Schokolade? Kalbsbraten? Bratkartoffeln?	*Do you like eating*	*meat? fish? fruit? chocolate? roast veal? fried potatoes?*
2. Trinken Sie gern	Tee mit Zitrone? schwarzen Kaffee? süßen Rotwein? herben Weißwein? helles Bier? dunkles Bier? kaltes Wasser? frische Milch?	*Do you like drinking*	*tea with lemon? black coffee? sweet red wine? dry white wine? light beer? dark beer? cold water? fresh milk?*

3. Sehen Sie gern	alte Kirchen? moderne Gebäude? schöne Gemälde? antike Statuen?			*Do you like* *seeing*	*old churches?* *modern buildings?* *beautiful paintings?* *antique statues?*		

4. Ja, ich (Nein, ich)	esse trinke sehe	ihn sie es sie	gern. (nicht gern).	*Yes, I like* *(No, I don't like)*	*eating* *drinking* *seeing*	*it (m.).* *it (f.).* *it (n.).* *them.*

5. Gehen Sie gern	ins Theater? ins Kino? in den Zirkus? im Park spazieren?	*Do you like* *going*	*to the theatre?* *to the cinema?* *to the circus?* *for a walk in the park?*

6. Wohin gehen Sie lieber,	ins Theater oder ins Konzert? in den Wald oder in den Park?	*Where do you* *prefer going,*	*to a theatre or to a* *concert?* *into the woods or* *into the park?*

ich gehe gern ich gehe lieber	ins Theater. ins Konzert. in den Wald.	*I like going* *I prefer going*	*to the*	*theatre.* *concert.* *woods.*

7. Was essen Sie lieber,	Äpfel oder Birnen? Kalbfleisch oder Rindfleisch? Blumenkohl oder Rosenkohl?	*What do you* *prefer eating,*	*apples or pears?* *veal or* *beef?* *cauliflower or* *brussels sprouts?*

Ich esse lieber Ich esse nicht gern	Äpfel. Birnen. Kalbfleisch. Rindfleisch. Blumenkohl. Rosenkohl.	*I prefer eating* *I don't like eating*	*apples.* *pears.* *veal.* *beef.* *cauliflower.* *brussels sprouts.*

8. Was kostet	die Melone? die Ananas? der Kürbis? die Kokosnuß?	*How much is*	*the melon?* *the pineapple?* *the pumpkin?* *the coconut?*

Was kosten	die Kirschen? die Pflaumen? die Erdbeeren? die Nüsse?	*How much are*	*the cherries?* *the plums?* *the strawberries?* *the nuts?*

Sechzig Pfennig Eine Mark zwanzig Zwei Mark fünfzig Fünfundzwanzig Mark	das Pfund. das Kilo. der Meter. der Liter.	60 *Pfennigs* 1,20 *Marks* 2,50 *Marks* 25 *Marks*	*a pound.* *a kilo.* *a metre.* *a litre.*

65

ε

9. Haben Sie nicht	billigere? größere? schönere? bessere?	_Haven't you got_	_cheaper ones?_ _bigger ones?_ _nicer ones?_ _better ones?_

10. Ist dies	der die das	billigste? größte? kleinste? längste? beste?	_Is this the_	_cheapest?_ _biggest?_ _smallest?_ _longest?_ _best?_

11. Sind dies die	billigsten? größten? schönsten? besten?	_Are these the_	_cheapest?_ _largest?_ _nicest?_ _best?_

12. Geben Sie mir bitte	ein halbes Pfund. einen halben Liter. dreieinhalb Meter. ein Viertel Pfund. sechs Liter. acht Pfund.	_Please give me_	_half a pound._ _half a litre._ _3½ metres._ _a quarter-pound._ _6 litres._ _8 pounds._

EXPLANATIONS

1. The comparative of _gern_, gladly, is _lieber_, preferably.

2. The superlative of adjectives ends in _-ste_. This ending changes to _-sten_ in all cases where adjectives take the ending _-n_, i.e. in the Accusative case (masculine singular only), in the Dative and Genitive cases (all genders, singular and plural) and in the plural preceded by _die, diese, jene, welche, meine, seine_, etc.

3. The singular is used instead of the plural in nouns expressing measurement or quantity, e.g. _drei Mark, zehn Pfennig, acht Pfund, sechs Meter, zwei Glas Bier, drei Stück Zucker_. This does not apply to nouns ending in _-e_, e.g. _zwei Tassen Tee, neun Flaschen Wein_.

4. _Herr_ and all masculine nouns ending in _-e_ add _-n_, and _Bär, Prinz, Student, Soldat_ and a few more add _-en_ in all cases, singular and plural, except the Nominative singular, e.g. _der Schwanz des Löwen_, the lion's tail; _Kennen Sie diesen Herrn?_ Do you know this gentleman?; _der Vater von diesem Jungen_, this boy's father.

Note from the last example that in the spoken language the Genitive case may be replaced by _von_ followed by the Dative case.

Lektion Zwölf

Er hängt den Anzug
in den Schrank.

Der Anzug hängt
in dem Schrank.

Sie legt ein Kissen
auf das Sofa.

Das Kissen liegt
auf dem Sofa.

Sie stellt die leeren
Milchflaschen vor die Tür.

Die leeren Milchflaschen
stehen vor der Tür.

DIE NEUE WOHNUNG[1]

(Fischers ziehen in ihre neue Wohnung ein.[2] Vor dem Hause steht ein großer Möbelwagen.[3] Zwei starke[4] Männer bringen die Möbel[3] herauf.[5])

Frau Fischer: Hierher[E] bitte ins Wohnzimmer. Stellen[E] Sie den Tisch in die Mitte,[6] das Sofa an die Wand[7] und den Sessel[8] vor das Fenster.

Erster Mann: Wohin[E] soll ich den Schreibtisch stellen?

Frau Fischer: Stellen Sie ihn da in die Ecke.[9]

Zweiter Mann *(bringt eine Lampe, ein Bild[10] und eine Vase)*: Wohin soll ich die Lampe stellen?

Frau Fischer: Stellen Sie die Lampe vor den Kamin.[11] Hängen Sie das Bild über den Kamin und stellen Sie die Vase auf den Tisch. So, das ist alles für dieses Zimmer. Sie können jetzt die Schlafzimmersachen[12] bringen.

(Frau Fischer geht ins Schlafzimmer. Herr Fischer kommt ins Wohnzimmer.)

Herr Fischer: Der Sessel vor dem Fenster gefällt[13] mir nicht. Der Sessel gehört[14] vor den Kamin. *(Er stellt den Sessel vor den Kamin.)*

Herr Fischer *(ruft[15] einen Mann)*: Kommen Sie doch bitte einen Augenblick[16] her. *(Er nimmt die Vase von dem Tisch und stellt sie auf den Kamin.)* Der Tisch in der Mitte gefällt mir nicht. Helfen[17] Sie mir bitte ihn vor das Fenster zu stellen. *(Sie stellen den Tisch vor das Fenster.)* So. Das Bild über dem Kamin gefällt mir auch nicht. Nehmen Sie es von dort weg[18] und hängen sie es über[E] den Schreibtisch.

---

[1] die Wohnung, –en, *flat; apartment.*
[2] einziehen, *to move in.*
[3] der Möbelwagen, –, *furniture van;* die Möbel (n. pl.), *furniture.*
[4] *strong.*
[5] *up.*
[6] *middle.*
[7] die Wand, ⸚e, *wall.*
[8] der Sessel, –, *armchair.*
[9] *corner.*
[10] das Bild, –er, *picture.*
[11] der Kamin, –e, *fireplace.*
[12] die Sache, –n, *thing.*
[13] gefallen, *to please.*
[14] gehören, *to belong.*
[15] rufen, *to call.*
[16] der Augenblick, –e, *moment.*
[17] helfen, *to help.*
[18] *away.*

1. Die Sachen sind | in / an / auf / unter / neben / vor / hinter | dem Schrank. / dem Koffer. / der Kommode. / der Schachtel. / den Koffern. / den Körben.
zwischen dem Schrank und der Kommode.

The things are | in / beside / on / under / near / in front of / behind | the wardrobe. / the suitcase. / the chest of drawers. / the box. / the suitcases. / the baskets.
between the wardrobe and the chest of drawers.

2. ich lege die Sachen | in / an / auf / unter / neben / vor / hinter | den Schrank. / den Koffer. / die Kommode. / die Hutschachtel. / die Koffer. / die Körbe.
zwischen den Schrank und die Kommode.

I put the things | into / beside / on / under / near / in front of / behind | the wardrobe. / the suitcase. / the chest of drawers. / the hat box. / the suitcases. / the baskets.
between the wardrobe and the chest of drawers.

3. ich stelle die leeren Milchflaschen | vor die Tür. / auf den Tisch. / in das Büffet.

Die leeren Milchflaschen stehen | vor der Tür. / auf dem Tisch. / in dem Büffet.

I put the empty milk bottles | before the door. / on the table. / into the sideboard.

The empty milk bottles stand | in front of the door. / on the table. / in the sideboard.

4. Stecken Sie | den Zettel / das Kleingeld / die Geldscheine | in die | Tasche. / Geldtasche. / Brieftasche.

Der Zettel / Das Kleingeld | steckt | in der | Westentasche. / Hosentasche. / Geldtasche.
Die Geldscheine stecken

Put the | note / small change / bank-notes | into the | pocket. / purse. / pocket-book.

The note / The change | is | in the | waistcoat-pocket. / trouser-pocket. / purse
The bank-notes are

5. Wohin legen Sie das Kissen?	*Where do you put the cushion?*
Ich lege es auf das Sofa.	*I put it on the sofa.*
Wo liegt das Kissen?	*Where is the cushion?*
Es liegt auf dem Sofa.	*It is on the sofa.*
Wohin stellen Sie die Stühle?	*Where do you put the chairs?*
Ich stelle sie an die Wand.	*I put them beside the wall.*
Wo stehen die Stühle?	*Where are the chairs?*
Sie stehen an der Wand.	*They are standing beside the wall.*
Wohin stecken Sie das Geld?	*Where do you put the money?*
Ich stecke es in die Geldtasche.	*I put it into the purse.*
Wo ist das Geld?	*Where is the money?*
Es ist in der Geldtasche.	*It is in the purse.*
Wohin hängen Sie die Bilder?	*Where do you hang the pictures?*
Ich hänge sie an die Wände.	*I hang them on the walls.*
Wo hängen die Bilder?	*Where do the pictures hang?*
Sie hängen an den Wänden im Wohnzimmer.	*They hang on the walls in the sitting room.*

EXPLANATIONS

1. in, *in*, *into*
   an, *by*, *at*
   auf, *on*
   unter, *under*
   vor, *before*
   hinter, *behind*
   über, *above*
   neben, *beside*
   zwischen, *between*

These nine prepositions may be followed by the noun in either the Dative or the Accusative case.
They are followed by the Dative case in answer to the question *wo?* where? and by the Accusative in answer to the question *wohin?* where to?

2. There are three German equivalents to the English verb 'to put'. *Stellen* is used for things which are placed upright, *legen* for things which lie flat and *stecken* in the sense of 'slip into'.

3. The difference formerly made in English between 'where' and 'whither' is still made in modern German: *wo*, where; *wohin*, whither, i.e. where to. There is also a difference in German, similar to that formerly made in English between 'here' and 'hither', 'there' and 'thither'.

Er ist nicht hier. He is not here. *Wer ist da?*[1] Who is there?

Er kommt oft her.[2] He often comes here. *Gehen Sie auch hin?*[3] Do you also go there?

---

[1] *or* dort.   [2] *or* hierher.   [3] *short for* dahin *or* dorthin.

Lektion Dreizehn

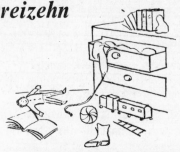

Wir haben Besuch gehabt.   Die Kinder haben gespielt.

Die Herren haben Zigarren   Die Damen haben Kaffee
geraucht und Wein getrunken.   getrunken und Kuchen gegessen.

FRITZ MACHT EINKÄUFE[1]

A: *Frau Fischer.*   B: *Fritz.*

A: Also Fritz, bring' ein großes Brot, ein halbes Pfund Butter,
beste Sorte, zwei Pfund Zucker und ein Dutzend Eier.[2] Vor-
sichtig[3] mit den Eiern, zerbrich[4] sie nicht. Hier sind zehn
Mark. Komm gleich[5] zurück.[6]

(*Fritz nimmt die Liste und das Geld und geht Einkäufe machen.
Nach[7] einer halben Stunde kommt er zurück.*)

A: Da bist[8] du endlich![9] Wo warst[10] du so lange?

[1] der Einkauf, ¨e, *purchase.*
[2] das Ei, –er, *egg.*
[3] *careful.*
[4] zerbrechen, *to break.*
[5] *immediately.*
[6] *back.*
[7] *after.*
[8] du bist, *you are (familiar form).*
[9] *at last.*
[10] du warst, *you were (familiar form).*

71

B: Die Geschäfte[1] waren voll.

A: Warum hast du nur ein kleines Brot gebracht?[F] Ich hatte dir doch gesagt,[E] du sollst[2] ein großes bringen.

B: Der Bäcker hat kein großes mehr gehabt. Deshalb[3] habe ich ein kleines genommen.[E]

A: Das ist doch[4] kein halbes Pfund Butter. Warum hast du nur ein Viertel Pfund gebracht?

B: Der Kaufmann[5] hat nicht mehr Butter gehabt.[E]

A: Warum hast du nur[6] drei Eier gekauft?[F] Ich hatte dir[7] doch gesagt, du sollst ein Dutzend bringen. Ein Ei ist zerbrochen.[8]

B: Er hat mir nicht mehr[9] gegeben.[E]

A: Nur ein halbes Pfund Zucker?

B: Der Kaufmann hat nicht mehr gehabt.

A: Wo ist der Rest des Geldes?

B: Ich hab' keins[F] mehr.

A: Du hast kein Geld mehr? Ich habe dir doch zehn Mark gegeben. Was hast du damit[10] gemacht?[11] Hast du das Geld verloren?[12]

B: Nein, ich habe es nicht verloren.

A: Hast du dir Schokolade gekauft?

B: Nein, ich habe mir nichts[F] gekauft.

A: Was hast du mit dem Geld gemacht?[11]

B: Ich habe mit den Kindern auf der Straße gespielt. Wir haben Ball gespielt und ich habe eine Fensterscheibe[13] zerbrochen. Der Mann hat gesagt, ich muß die Fensterscheibe bezahlen.[14] Er hat einen großen Stock[15] gehabt, und ich habe ihm fünf Mark gegeben. Da hab' ich nicht mehr genug[16] Geld für alle Einkäufe gehabt.

[1] das Geschäft, –e, *shop; business*.
[2] du sollst, *you shall (familiar form)*.
[3] *therefore*.
[4] *but; yes; indeed (added for emphasis)*.
[5] *grocer*.
[6] *only*.
[7] *to you (familiar form in the Dative case)*.
[8] *broken*.
[9] *more*.
[10] *with it*.
[11] machen, *to make, to do*.
[12] verlieren, *to lose*.
[13] die Fensterscheibe, –n, *window pane*.
[14] *pay*.
[15] der Stock, ¨-e, *stick*.
[16] *enough*.

English

1.

I	waited or I have	He	has	waited.
He	played	She		played.
She	worked			worked.
We	slept	We	have	slept.
You	wrote	You		written.
They	read	They		read.

2.

Have	you	seen him?	or *Did you see him?* etc.
	we	heard that?	
	they	already eaten?	
Has	he	had something to drink?	
	she	taken some?	
		done it?	
Have I		lost them?	
		found that?	

3.

I	didn't[1]	bring	the suitcase.
He		fetch	it (m.).
She		see	the parcel.
		take	it (n.).
We		find	the flowers.
You		lose	them.
They		forget	

4.

I	saw	Herr Schmidt	here.
You	spoke to	him	there.
	left	Frau Berger	upstairs.
	met	her	downstairs.
	looked for	the children	outside.
		them	inside.
			in Vienna.
			in the street.
			in the garden.

[1] or *haven't brought*, etc.

German

1.

ich habe	hat	gewartet.
er		gespielt.
sie		gearbeitet.
wir	haben	geschlafen.
Sie		geschrieben.
sie		gelesen.

2.

Haben	Sie wir sie	ihn gesehen?
		das gehört?
Hat	er sie	schon gegessen?
		etwas getrunken?
		welche genommen?
		es getan?
Habe ich		sie verloren?
		das gefunden?

3.

ich habe	hat	den Koffer	nicht	gebracht.
er		ihn		geholt.
sie		das Paket		gesehen.
wir	haben	es		genommen.
Sie		die Blumen		gefunden.
sie		sie		verloren.
				vergessen.

4.

ich habe	Herrn Schmidt	hier	gesehen.
du hast^E	ihn	dort	gesprochen.
ihr habt^E	Frau Berger	oben	gelassen.
Sie haben	sie	unten	getroffen.
	die Kinder	draußen	gesucht.
	sie	drinnen	
		in Wien	
		auf der Straße	
		im Garten	

5.

What did	you he she	do	today? yesterday?

		I he she	went for a walk.
In the morning			had a bath.
In the forenoon			wrote letters.
In the afternoon		we they	visited the cathedral.
In the evening			listened to the wireless.
Before the midday meal			played the piano.
After the evening meal			

Was	haben Sie hat er sie	heute gestern	getan?

	morgens	einen Spaziergang gemacht.
ich habe	vormittags	ein Bad genommen.
er hat	nachmittags	Briefe geschrieben.
sie	abends	den Dom besichtigt.
wir haben	vor dem Mittagessen	Radio gehört.
sie	nach dem Abendessen	Klavier gespielt.

6.

I You	bought	the bread at the baker's.
		the meat at the butcher's.
		the salad at the greengrocer's.
		the pears at the fruiterer's.
		the pastries at the pastrycook's.
		the sugar at the grocer's.
		the butter in the dairy.
		the herrings at the fish market.

ich habe	das Brot beim Bäcker	gekauft.
du hast	das Fleisch beim Fleischer	
ihr habt	den Salat beim Gemüsehändler	
Sie haben	die Birnen beim Obsthändler	
	die Torten beim Konditor	
	den Zucker in der Kolonialwaren-handlung	
	die Butter in der Milchhandlung	
	die Heringe auf dem Fischmarkt	

7.

Who has Have you	hung the overcoat in the wardrobe?
	put the watch on the table?
	put the umbrella in the corner?
	led the dog into the street?
	taken the car into the garage?

Wer hat	den Mantel in den Schrank gehängt?
Haben Sie	die Uhr auf den Tisch gelegt?
Hast du^E	den Schirm in die Ecke gestellt?
Habt ihr^E	den Hund auf die Straße geführt?
	das Auto in die Garage gebracht?

8.

Did you	see take find have buy	one (m.)? none (m.)? one (f.)? none (f.)? one (n.)? none (n.)? nothing?

Hast du^E	einen	gesehen?
Habt ihr^E	keinen	genommen?
Haben Sie	eine	gefunden?
	keine	gehabt?
	eins	gekauft?
	keins	
	nichts	

74

1. What happened in the past is in conversational German usually expressed by the Perfect tense. This is formed by the auxiliary *haben* with the past participle of the verb. A few verbs, which are mentioned in the following lesson, use the auxiliary *sein*.

The past participle normally has the prefix *ge-* and ends in either *-t* or *-en*, e.g. *gewohnt, gehabt, gesehen, gegessen*.

2. There is practically no difference in meaning between *ich nahm* (the Imperfect of *nehmen*, to take) and *ich habe genommen* (the Perfect). Both express what happened or has happened, but the Perfect is more usual in conversation. For the use of the Imperfect see Lesson XV, Explanation 2.

3. When one is talking to more than one child, near relative or intimate friend they are addressed as *ihr*, which is the plural of *du*. The verb in connection with *ihr* ends in *-t*: *ihr kommt, ihr nehmt, ihr habt*, etc. The only exception is *ihr seid*, the plural of *du bist*, you are.

4. Corresponding to the three forms of the verb with *Sie*, *du* and *ihr*, there are three forms of the Imperative:

FAMILIAR FORM		POLITE FORM	
Singular	*Plural*	*Singular and Plural*	
komm!	kommt!	kommen Sie!	*come!*
schau!	schaut!	schauen Sie!	*look!*
nimm!	nehmt!	nehmen Sie!	*take!*
sei pünktlich!	seid pünktlich!	seien Sie pünktlich!	*be punctual!*

5. The plural of *dein(e)* is *euer* (*eure*): *euer Vater, eure Mutter, eure Eltern*.

6. The plural of both *dir* and *dich* is *euch*, e.g.

Gehört dies dir?	*Does this belong to you* (sing.)?
Gehört dies euch?	*Does this belong to you* (pl.)?
Ich habe dich gestern gesehen.	*I saw you* (sing.) *yesterday.*
Ich habe euch gestern gesehen.	*I saw you* (pl.) *yesterday.*

Lektion Vierzehn

Der Junge klettert
auf einen Apfelbaum.

Er ist auf den
Apfelbaum geklettert.

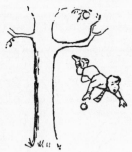

Er fällt vom Baum

Er ist vom Baum gefallen.

EIN BESUCH

A: *Herr Fischer.* B: *Frau Fischer.* C: *Georg.* D: *Fritz.*
E: *das Dienstmädchen.*[1]

*(Georg ist mit dem Autobus zur Ahornallee gefahren[2] und hat gleich
das Haus No. 28 gefunden. Er ist mit dem Fahrstuhl[3] in den dritten
Stock[4] hinaufgefahren und hat auf die Klingel[5] neben der Wohnungs-
tür gedrückt.[6] Das Dienstmädchen öffnet.)*

[1] das Dienstmädchen, *maid.*
[2] fahren, *to drive.*
[3] *lift.*

[4] *short for* das Stockwerk, –e, *floor, storey.*
[5] die Klingel, –, *bell.*
[6] dr cken, *to press.*

76

C: Wohnt[1] hier Herr Fischer?

E: Ja. Wen[2] darf[3] ich melden?[4]

C: Georg Heimann. Hier ist meine Karte.

E: Wollen Sie bitte hier Platz nehmen.

(*Sie öffnet die Tür des Salons[5] und läßt[6] Georg eintreten.[7] Dann bringt sie die Karte ins Wohnzimmer und gibt sie Herrn Fischer.*)

E: Der Herr möchte[8] Sie sprechen.

A (*zu seiner Frau*): Das ist der Amerikaner, den[9] wir im Zug getroffen[10] haben. (*Zum Dienstmädchen*) Bitten[11] Sie den Herrn hier herein.

E (*zu Georg*): Wollen Sie mir bitte folgen.[12]

A: Es ist schön, daß Sie uns in Berlin besuchen.[13]

C: Ich hoffe,[14] Sie nicht zu stören.[15]

A: Aber nein. Sie sind sehr willkommen.

B: Wie gefällt[16] es Ihnen in Berlin?

C: Danke. Es gefällt mir sehr.

B: Haben Sie schon die Oper besucht?

C: Ich bin gestern abend in der Oper gewesen. Ich habe *Figaros Hochzeit*[17] gesehen. Es hat mir sehr gefallen. Vorgestern[18] bin ich im Theater gewesen.

A: In welchem Theater sind Sie gewesen?

C: Im Staatstheater.

B: Was haben Sie gesehen?

C: Shakespeares *Sommernachtstraum*.

B: Wie hat es Ihnen gefallen?

C: Es hat mir sehr gut gefallen.

---

[1] wohnen, *to live; to dwell.*
[2] *whom.*
[3] *may.*
[4] *announce.*
[5] der Salon, –s. *drawing room.*
[6] lassen, *to let.*
[7] *enter.*
[8] *would like.*
[9] *whom.*
[10] treffen, *to meet.*
[11] *ask.*
[12] folgen, *to follow.*
[13] *visit.*
[14] *hope.*
[15] *disturb.*
[16] Wie gefällt es Ihnen? *How do you like it?* (*lit. how does it please you?*)
[17] die Hochzeit, –en, *wedding; marriage.*
[18] *the day before yesterday.*

FLUENCY PRACTICE

1.

ich bin — er ist — sie / wir — Sie — sie sind	gestern vorgestern Montag oft manchmal selten nie	ins Theater ins Kino ins Konzert tanzen baden schwimmen Eislaufen	gegangen.
I — He — She / We — You — They	went	yesterday the day before yesterday on Monday often sometimes seldom never	to the theatre. to the cinema. to the concert. dancing. bathing. swimming. skating.

2.

Sind Sie — Bist du — Seid ihr	zu Fuß mit dem Autobus mit der Straßenbahn mit der Eisenbahn mit der Untergrundbahn auf dem Fahrrad auf dem Motorrad	hierher zur Schule zur Stunde	gekommen?
Did you come	here to the school to the lesson	on foot? by bus? by tram? by rail? by the Underground? on a bicycle? on a motorcycle?	

3.

Ist — er / sie — Sind — Sie / sie	mit der Eisenbahn mit dem Schiff mit dem Flugzeug mit dem Auto	nach Österreich nach der Schweiz nach den Vereinigten Staaten	gefahren?
Did — he / she — you / they — go	to Austria? to Switzerland? to the United States?	by rail? by boat? by air? by car?	

4.

Wie lange sind Sie — bist du — seid ihr	dort im Bad auf der Eisbahn in Frankreich in der Türkei in den Kolonien	geblieben?	
How long did you stay	there? in the bath? on the skating rink? in France? in Turkey? in the colonies?		

78

5.

Wir sind			gewesen.
gestern	hier		
vorgestern	dort		
letzte Woche	in Wien		
vor vierzehn Tagen	in Österreich		
vor einiger Zeit	in der Schweiz		
vor langer Zeit	in den Alpen		
vor einigen Wochen	in den Vereinigten Staaten		
vor drei Monaten			
vor einem Jahr			
vor vielen Jahren			

We were	here		yesterday.
	there		the day before yesterday.
	in Vienna		last week.
	in Austria		a fortnight ago.
	in Switzerland		some time ago.
	in the Alps		a long time ago.
	in the U.S.A.		some weeks ago.
			three months ago.
			a year ago.
			many years ago.

6.

Ich bin / Wir sind		geblieben.
nur kurze Zeit	dort	
längere Zeit	in Basel	
eine Woche	in der Schweiz	
vierzehn Tage		
drei Wochen		
neun Monate		
einige Jahre		

I / We	stayed	there	only a short while.
		in Basle	for some time.
		in Switzerland	one week.
			a fortnight.
			three weeks.
			nine months.
			several years.

7.

Wann	sind Sie / ist er / sie	geboren?

er / sie	ist	am ersten April	geboren.
		am dritten Juli	gestorben.
		am zehnten Juni	

When	were you / was he / she	born?

He / She	was born / died	on the 1st of April.
		on the 3rd of July.
		on the 10th of June.

1. The past participles of verbs denoting either change of place (to go, to come, etc.) or change of condition (to become, to be born, to die, etc.) form Perfects with *sein*, to be.

This also applies to the past participles *gewesen*, been, and *geblieben*, remained.

2. *Gehen* is 'to go' only in the sense of 'to walk' or 'to leave'. To go by bus, train, car, etc. is *fahren*.

3. The second item in every German sentence *must* be a verb. Compare the following and note that with whatever part of the sentence you start, the verb follows as the second part:

Ich GEHE *heute zu meinem Onkel.*
Zu meinem Onkel GEHE *ich heute.*
Heute GEHE *ich zu meinem Onkel.*

The only exceptions to the above rule are questions which commence with the verb, and Imperatives, e.g.

GEHEN *Sie heute ins Theater?* Are you going to the theatre today?

KOMMEN *Sie bitte herein.* Please come in.

4. The past participle is at the end of the sentence and the auxiliary (unless it starts a question) becomes the second item, e.g.

Wir SIND *gestern ins Theater gegangen.* We went to the theatre yesterday.

SIND *Sie auch dort gewesen?* Were you there, too?

Lektion Fünfzehn

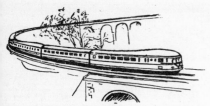
das Auto

der Omnibus

die Eisenbahn

das Motorrad

die Bergbahn

der Motorroller

das Fahrrad

81

F

A: *Herr Fischer*. B: *Frau Fischer*. C: *Georg*. D: *Fritz*.
(*Frau Fischer hat Georg zum Abendessen eingeladen[1].*)

B: Noch etwas[2] Salat, Herr Heimann?

C: Gern. Er schmeckt[3] großartig.[4]

A: Wie finden Sie den Wein?

C: Er ist ausgezeichnet.[5]

B: Sind Sie schon viel in Europa gereist?[6]

C: Nur in die Schweiz.

D: Wir sind letztes[7] Jahr auch in der Schweiz gewesen. Wir waren auf dem Rigi. Wir sind mit einem Schiff von Luzern nach Weggis gefahren und dann mit der Bergbahn* hinaufgefahren.

C: Ich bin aber zu Fuß hinaufgegangen.

B: Wie lange hat es gedauert,[8] zu Fuß hinaufzugehen?

C: Etwa[9] drei Stunden.

A: Mit der Bahn hat es nur eine halbe Stunde gedauert und war weniger anstrengend.[10]

B (*hat dem Mädchen geklingelt[11]*): Sie können den Nachtisch[12] servieren.

A: Was gibt's[13] zum Nachtisch?

B: Erdbeeren mit Schlagsahne.[14]

(*Das Mädchen bringt den Nachtisch, und Frau Fischer legt jedem eine Portion auf,[15] außer[16] Fritz.*)

B (*zu Fritz*): Du hast deine Portion schon gehabt. (*Zu Georg*) Der Bengel[17] hat in der Küche[18] genascht.[19]

---

[1] einladen, *to invite.*
[2] noch etwas, *some more.*
[3] schmecken, *to taste.*
[4] *magnificent(ly).*
[5] *excellent(ly).*
[6] reisen, *to travel.*
[7] *last.*
[8] *How long did it take? from* dauern, *to last.*
[9] *about.*
[10] *strenuous.*
[11] klingeln, *to ring the bell.*

[12] der Nachtisch, –e, *dessert.*
[13] Was gibt es? *What is there? What's on?*
[14] die Schlagsahne, –n, *whipped cream.*
[15] auflegen, *to put on; to serve.*
[16] *except.*
[17] der Bengel–, *rascal.*
[18] die Küche, –n, *kitchen.*
[19] naschen, *to help oneself to dainties (esp. without permission).*

C: Ich kann das verstehen.[1] Die Versuchung[2] war zu stark.[3] Es
   schmeckt ausgezeichnet. Wollen Sie ihm nicht verzeihen?[4]
B: Weil[5] Herr Heimann mich bittet, will ich dir verzeihen. Da
   hast du deine Portion.
D: Oh, fein!

[1] *understand.*   [4] *forgive.*
[2] *temptation.*   [5] *because.*
[3] *strong.*

EXPLANATIONS

1. Ordinal numbers take the ending *-te* from 2nd to 19th, and
-ste from 20th onwards. There are special words for 1st and 3rd:
erste and *dritte*. The ordinal numbers are adjectives and so take
the usual endings, e.g. *am vierten Juli*, on the fourth of July.

2. The Imperfect is used to express (*a*) what was, (*b*) what was
happening, (*c*) what used to happen.

3. In a sentence containing both an expression of time and of
place, time precedes place, e.g. *wir gehen heute abend ins Theater*,
we are going to the theatre tonight.

FLUENCY PRACTICE

1. Waren Sie mal in der Schweiz?		*Have you ever been to Switzerland?*
Wann waren Sie dort?		*When were you there?*
Wo wohnten Sie?		*Where did you live?*
Was taten Sie dort?		*What did you do there?*
Wie lange blieben Sie dort?		*How long did you stay there?*
Haben Sie Luzern besucht?		*Did you visit Lucerne?*
Haben Sie die Alpen gesehen?		*Did you see the Alps?*
Sind Sie auf die Berge gestiegen, oder sind Sie mit der Drahtseilbahn hinaufgefahren?		*Did you climb the mountains or did you go up by the cable railway?*

2. Welcher Tag	ist	heute?	*What day*	*is*	*today?*
Der wievielste		morgen?	*What date*		*tomorrow?*
		übermorgen?			*the day after tomorrow?*

Welcher Tag	war	gestern?	*What day*	*was*	*yesterday?*
Der wievielste		vorgestern?	*What date*		*the day before yesterday?*

3.

German:

		der	
Heute	ist	erste	Januar.
Morgen		zweite	Februar.
Übermorgen		dritte	März.
		vierte	April.
Gestern	war	fünfte	Mai.
Vorgestern		sechste	Juni.
		siebente	Juli.
		achte	August.
		zwanzigste	September.
		einundzwanzigste	Oktober.
		zweiundzwanzigste	November.
		dreißigste	Dezember.

		Sonntag	hier.
Heute	ist	Montag	dort.
	war	Dienstag	
		Mittwoch	
		Donnerstag	
		Freitag	
		Sonnabend[1]	

English:

		the	(of)
Today	is	first	January.
Tomorrow		second	February.
The day after tomorrow		third	March.
		fourth	April.
Yesterday	was	fifth	May.
The day before yesterday		sixth	June.
		seventh	July.
		eighth	August.
		twentieth	September.
		twenty-first	October.
		twenty-second	November.
		thirtieth	December.

		Sunday	here
	is	Monday	there
	was	Tuesday	
		Wednesday	
		Thursday	
		Friday	
		Saturday	

[1] Samstag in Southern Germany, Switzerland and Austria.

4.

German:

			hier.
ich	war	oft	dort.
er		selten	
sie		manchmal	
es		jede Woche	
		jeden Monat	
wir	waren	jedes Jahr	
Sie		dreimal im Jahr	
sie		regelmäßig	

English:

				here
I	was	used to be	often.	there
He			seldom.	
She			sometimes.	
It			every week.	
			each month.	
We	were	used to be	each year.	
You			three times a year.	
They			regularly.	

84

5.

ich	wartete	fünf Minuten	in Ihrem Zimmer.
er	arbeitete	eine viertel Stunde	im Garten.
sie	schrieb		in meinem Büro.
	saß	eine halbe Stunde	in der Eingangshalle.
	blieb	drei Stunden	im Wohnzimmer.
		den ganzen Tag	
		einige Zeit	

wir	warteten
Sie	arbeiteten
sie	schrieben
	saßen
	blieben

I	was	waiting[1]	five minutes	in your room.
He		working	for a quarter of an hour	in the garden.
She		writing		in my office.
		sitting	for half an hour	in the entrance hall.
		staying	three hours	in the living room.
			the whole day	
			for some time	

We	were
You	
They	

[1] or *used to wait*, etc.

6.

ich	sah	ihn	hier.
er	sprach	sie	dort.
sie	hörte	es	in der Schule.
	fand	sie	im Büro.
	hatte	oft	
		manchmal	
		jeden Tag	
		jede Woche	

wir	sahen
Sie	sprachen
sie	hörten
	fanden
	hatten

I	used to	see	him	here	often.
He		speak to	her	there	sometimes.
She		hear	it	at school	every day.
		find	them	in the office	every week.
		have			

We	
You	
They	

7.

ich	kam	jeden Tag	hierher.
er	ging	jede Woche	dorthin.
sie	fuhr	jeden Monat	nach Zürich.
es		jedes Jahr	an die See.
		sehr oft	in die Stadt.
		hin und wieder	
		von Zeit zu Zeit	
		immer	

wir	kamen
Sie	gingen
sie	fuhren

I	used to	come	every day	here.
He		go	every week	there.
She		travel	every month	to Zürich.
It			every year	to the seaside.
			very often	to town.
			now and then	
			from time to time	
			always	

We	
You	
They	

Lektion Sechzehn

Es regnet:
(der Herr macht den
Regenschirm auf).

Es ist kalt:
(das Mädel reibt
sich die Hände).

Es ist heiß:
(der dicke Herr
wischt sich die Stirn).

Die Sonne scheint:
(man nimmt ein Sonnenbad).

Es ist windig:
(der Wind hat der Dame den
Hut vom Kopf gerissen).

Es schneit:
(die Kinder werfen Schneebälle).

A: *Herr Fischer.*   B: *Frau Fischer.*   C: *Georg.*   D: *Fritz.*

B: Wie lange werden Sie in Deutschland bleiben?[1]

C: Ich werde noch zwei Wochen bleiben, aber nicht die ganze[2] Zeit[3] in Berlin.

A: Wo werden Sie noch hinfahren?

C: Ich werde eine Woche in Süddeutschland bleiben und eine Woche am Rhein.

B: Werden Sie mit dem Schiff auf dem Rhein fahren?

C: Ich werde bis Mainz mit der Eisenbahn[4] fahren und dann mit dem Dampfer[5] auf dem Rhein.

A: Werden Sie Köln besuchen?[6]

C: Ich werde nur einen halben Tag in Köln bleiben, um den Dom[7] zu besichtigen.[8] In Köln werde ich einen Freund aus Amerika treffen,[9] und wir werden zusammen mit seinem Auto nach Frankreich fahren und Paris besuchen.

D: Werden Sie auch auf den Eiffelturm[10] steigen?[11]

C: Gewiß[12] werde ich auch auf den Eiffelturm steigen.

A: Wie lange werden Sie in Frankreich bleiben?

C: Nur einige[13] Tage. Von dort werden wir nach London fliegen.[14]

B: In London soll[15] es doch so neblig[16] sein.

C: Wenn es neblig ist, werden wir nicht fliegen können.[17]

B: Ich hoffe,[18] Sie werden gutes Wetter[19] haben.

C: Danke schön! (*Schaut*[20] *auf die Uhr.*) Es ist aber Zeit, daß ich gehe. (*Steht auf.*) Ich danke[21] Ihnen für den angenehmen[22] Abend und das schöne Abendessen.

---

[1] *stay.*
[2] *whole.*
[3] die Zeit, –en, *time.*
[4] die Eisenbahn, –en, *railway.*
[5] der Dampfer, –, *steamer.*
[6] *visit.*
[7] der Dom, –e, *cathedral.*
[8] *see; inspect.*
[9] *meet.*
[10] der Turm, ⸚e, *tower.*
[11] steigen, *to go up.*

[12] *certain(ly).*
[13] *a few.*
[14] *fly.*
[15] soll sein, *is supposed to be.*
[16] *foggy.*
[17] *be able.*
[18] hoffen, *to hope.*
[19] das Wetter, *weather.*
[20] schauen, *to look; to glance.*
[21] danken, *to thank.*
[22] angenehm, *pleasant.*

B: Wir danken Ihnen für den Besuch.[1] Kommen Sie bald[2] wieder.
Wir werden Sie gern bei uns sehen.

[1] der Besuch, –e, *visit.*　　　　　　　　　　　　　　[2] *soon.*

EXPLANATIONS

1. The Future tense is formed with the auxiliary *werden* and the Infinitive. The Infinitive is placed at the end of the sentence and the auxiliary (unless it starts a question) takes the second place in the order of words.

2. Möchten Sie? *Would you like to?*
Könnten Sie? *Could you?*
are more polite than *Wollen Sie?* and *Können Sie?*

3. In subordinate clauses the verb is at the end of the clause, e.g.
Er kann nicht kommen, weil er krank ist. *He cannot come because he is ill.*
Sie sagt, daß sie nach Frankreich fahren wird. *She says that she will go to France.*
Wenn es neblig ist, werden wir nicht fliegen können. *If it is foggy, we shall not be able to fly.*

4. The Infinitive ends in *-en*. A few Infinitives end in *-n*, e.g. *tun*, to do; *radeln*, to cycle; *ärgern*, to annoy. With such verbs all forms of the verb normally ending in *-en* drop the *e*:
Was tun Sie? *What are you doing?*

5. Am Sonntag stehen wir später auf. *On Sunday we get up later.*
Der März war dieses Jahr sehr kalt. *March was very cold this year.*
Im Sommer fahren wir an die See. *In summer we go to the seaside.*

Days, months and seasons are masculine in German. Note also the use of the definite article in connection with them.

FLUENCY PRACTICE

1.

ich werde		eine Reise machen.	im Sommer
er	wird	ins Gebirge fahren.	im Winter
sie		an die See fahren.	im Frühling
es		aufs Land fahren.	in den Ferien
		einen hohen Berg besteigen.	zu Ostern
wir	werden	das Schloß besichtigen.	zu Pfingsten
Sie		einen Ausflug machen.	zu Weihnachten
sie		Österreich besuchen.	

I shall		make a journey	in summer.
He	will	go to the mountains	in winter.
She		go to the seaside	in spring.
It		go to the country	in the holidays.
		climb a high mountain	at Easter.
We	shall	visit the castle	at Whitsun.
You	will	make an excursion	at Christmas.
They		visit Austria	

2.

Morgen abend	werde ich	dort	sein.
Dienstag früh	wird	in Wien	
Sonntag nachmittag	er	an der See	
In einer Woche	sie	auf dem Lande	
In vierzehn Tagen	es	im Gebirge	
Nächste Woche	werden	bei meinem Onkel	
Nächsten Monat	wir	bei meiner Tante	
Nächstes Jahr	Sie	bei meinen Eltern	
Bald	sie		

Tomorrow night	I shall	be	there.
Tuesday morning	he	will	in Vienna.
Sunday afternoon	she		at the seaside.
In a week's time	it		in the country.
In a fortnight			in the mountains.
Next week	we shall		at my uncle's.
Next month	you	will	at my aunt's.
Next year	they		with my parents.
Soon			

3.

Werden	Sie	heute abend	ins Theater	gehen?
	wir	Sonntag nachmittag	ins Kino	
	sie	nächsten Dienstag	ins Konzert	
		nächste Woche	in den Zirkus	
Wird	er	in diesem Jahr	in die Oper	
	sie			

Will	you	go	to the theatre	tonight?
	we		to the cinema	Sunday afternoon?
	they		to the concert	next Tuesday?
			to the circus	next week?
Will	he		to the opera	this year
	she			

4.

Werden Sie		tanzen	gehen?
Wann werden Sie		baden	
Mit wem werden Sie	wirst du	schwimmen	
	werdet ihr	wandern	
		~~eislaufen~~ eis laufen	
		bergsteigen	

Will you	go	dancing?
When will you		bathing?
With whom will you		swimming?
		hiking?
		skating?
		mountaineering?

5.

English

I He She It We They You	can will must would (not) like to	(not)	speak German. dance the polka. read German books. sing German songs. write German letters. play tennis. learn to play the piano. go skating. do so much.

German

ich er sie es wir sie Sie	kann will muß möchte können wollen müssen möchten	(nicht)	deutsch sprechen. Polka tanzen. deutsche Bücher lesen. deutsche Lieder singen. deutsche Briefe schreiben. Tennis spielen. Klavier spielen lernen. eislaufen gehen. so viel tun.

6.

English

Can Could I he she Can Could we they Would you like to	have	something to eat? something to drink? something to read? lunch now? dinner soon? breakfast at eight? coffee in the garden? a bottle of red wine? eggs and bacon? Frankfurt sausages? strawberries with cream?

Could you Would you	please	give me a light? lend me your newspaper? tell me what time it is? tell me where the nearest letter-box is? tell me how I get from here to the station?

German

Kann Könnte ich er sie Können Könnten wir sie Möchten Sie Möchtest du Möchtet ihr	etwas zu essen etwas zu trinken etwas zu lesen jetzt das Mittagessen bald das Abendessen das Frühstück um acht den Kaffee im Garten eine Flasche Rotwein Eier und Speck Frankfurter Würstchen Erdbeeren mit Schlagsahne	haben?

Könnten Sie Würden Sie	mir bitte	Feuer geben? Ihre Zeitung leihen? sagen, wieviel Uhr es ist? sagen, wo der nächste Briefkasten ist? sagen, wie ich von hier zum Bahnhof komme?

PRONUNCIATION PRACTICE[1]

1. der Ball, die Hand, das Lamm   der Hahn, das Schaf, die Saat
   der Stern, das Bett, das Nest   das Reh, der Esel, die See
   das Bild, die Milch, der Fisch   der Stier, die Biene, die Ziege
   der Frosch, der Topf, das Loch   das Boot, das Ohr, die Krone
   der Hund, der Fuchs, die Tulpe   die Kuh, der Zug, der Kuchen

2. die Tasse—das Täßchen, die Katze—das Kätzchen, der Arm—
   der Ärmel, der Bär, die Säge, der Käse, der Käfig, das Rad—die
   Räder
   der Löffel, zwölf, die Glocke—das Glöckchen, der Korb—die
   Körbe, die Flöte, die Möhre, der Löwe—die Löwin, der Vogel—
   die Vögel
   die Hütte, fünf, die Mütze, die Bürste, der Hund—das Hünd-
   chen, der Strumpf—die Strümpfe
   die Tür, der Hügel, der Hut—die Hüte, die Kuh—die Kühe,
   der Müller—die Mühle

3. das Ei, das Kleid, das Schwein, die Peitsche
   der Baum, das Auto, der Taucher, die Schaukel
   das Kreuz, die Eule, neun
   der Baum—die Bäume, das Haus—die Häuser
   die Küche, das Licht, der Becher, die Milch, die Eichel
   acht, die Nacht, der Koch, der Kuchen
   das Buch—die Bücher, das Dach—die Dächer, das Loch—die
   Löcher

4. die Sonne, die Rose, der Esel, der Sand, sechs
   die Straße, der Fluß, die Nuß, das Wasser, das Messer, der
   Schlüssel
   das Glas—die Gläser, der Fuß—die Füße, das Haus—die
   Häuser, die Nuß—die Nüsse
   der Zahn—die Zähne, das Zimmer, die Katze, der Arzt, zwei,
   zwölf

[1] Filmstrips and records available from Camera Talks, 31 North Row, London, W.1.

5. das Feld, der Affe, der Vater, der Vogel
   der Wald, das Wasser, das Klavier, die Violine
   der Pudel, der Apfel, der Lappen
   der Besen, die Gabel, der Schrubber
   der Korb, der Krebs, das Obst
   das Pferd, die Pflaume, der Pfirsich

6. die Tanne, die Tonne, das Theater, der Thron
   das Dach, der Adler, das Ruder, die Räder
   das Rad, die Hand, die Stadt
   der Garten, das Geld, der Wagen, der Regen
   der Tag, der Ring, der Krug, der Sack
   die Axt, die Hexe, der Ochse, sechs
   die Quelle, die Qualle, die Quittung, bequem

7. zehn, sehen, Zone, Sonne, Sohn, Söhne, Zaun, Zäune, Ofen,
   offen, Lamm, lahm, Feld, fehlt, Herr, Heer, im, ihm, List, liest,
   Mitte, Miete, hacken, Haken, satt, Saat, Kissen, küssen, Biene,
   Bühne, vier, für, liegen, lügen, kennen, können, Mieter, Mütter,
   schießen, Schüsse, Lift, lüften, Schwert, schwört
   ich, ach, dich, doch, rechnen, rauchen, sprechen, spricht,
   Sprache, Recht, Rache, frech, Fracht, China, Richard, Koch,
   Köchin, Küche
   rot, rechts, Rabe, grabe, Rose, groß, Raum, braun, Braten,
   Garten, Rückreise, Radfahrer, irren, klirren, Karren, arbeiten,
   Fahrrad

8. Fischers Fritz fischt frische Fische.
   Sieben Schneeschipper schippen siebenundsiebzig Schippen
   Schnee.
   Bürsten mit schwarzen Borsten bürsten besser als Bürsten mit
   weißen Borsten.
   Dreiunddreißig römische Ritter ritten dreiunddreißigmal um das
   römische Rathaus herum. Sie ritten und ritten und kamen nicht
   'rum.
   Der Potsdamer Postkutscher putzt den Potsdamer Postkutsch-
   kasten.

EXERCISES

A. Answer all questions both affirmatively and negatively:

1. Sprechen Sie	deutsch?	2. Essen Sie	Fisch?
Spricht Ihr	englisch?	Ißt Ihre	Fleisch?
Bruder	französisch?	Schwester	Käse?
	spanisch?		Wurst?
	russisch?		Obst?
	italienisch?		Gemüse?
			Schokolade?

3. Rauchen Sie?—Spielen Sie Tennis?—Trinken Sie Bier?—
Heißen Sie Karl?—Heißt Ihre Schwester Anna?—Heißt
Ihr Bruder Fritz?

B. Answer all possible questions:

Wie heißt	Ihr Vater?
Wie alt ist	Ihre Mutter?
	Ihr Bruder?
	Ihre Schwester?

Wie heißen Sie?

C. Say in German:
1. Is this tea or coffee?
2. This is not tea.
3. Please wait.
4. You eat fish, don't you?
5. She drinks beer, doesn't she?
6. Don't drink that.
7. Do you speak French?
8. No, I don't.
9. Does your husband drink coffee?
10. Are you coming now?
11. Yes, I am.
12. Is your brother eating now?
13. Does your sister play tennis?
14. What are you reading?
15. Do you smoke?

A. Answer both affirmatively and negatively, replacing all nouns by pronouns:

1. Ist

der Hut	gut?
der Kragen	schön?
die Bluse	zu klein?
das Kleid	nicht zu groß?
die Krawatte	nicht zu hell?
das Taschentuch	

2. Sind

die Schuhe	neu?
die Handschuhe	blau?
die Socken	grau?
die Strümpfe	groß genug?
die Hosen	nicht zu weit?
die Röcke	nicht zu eng?

3.

Sind Sie	krank?
Ist dieser Herr	müde?
Ist diese Dame	einverstanden?
Sind diese Herren	aus Berlin?
Sind diese Damen	
Sind diese Kinder	

B. Replace the nouns in italics by pronouns:

1. *Dieses Kleid* ist zu kurz.
2. *Diese Lampe* ist zu niedrig.
3. Ist *der Schrank* neu?
4. *Die Kinder* schauen durch das Fenster.
5. *Dieser Platz* ist besetzt.
6. *Die Schokolade* ist gut.
7. Trinkt *Ihre Frau* Wein?
8. Sind *die Fenster* offen?

C. Give the plural of:

1. Das Kind.
2. Der Rock.
3. Der Mantel.
4. Der Hut.
5. Die Jacke.
6. Der Platz.
7. Das Fenster.
8. Der Schrank.
9. Die Gabel.
10. Der Ofen.
11. Der Strumpf.
12. Die Handtasche.

D. Say in German:

1. Is this your spoon?
2. The little spoon is too short.
3. The new chairs are too high.
4. These blue gloves are too small.
5. Are you tired?
6. Who is that woman?
7. She is my sister.
8. Is she ill?
9. Is this the new lamp?
10. Isn't it too dark?
11. Aren't these dresses too short?
12. They are too tight, aren't they?
13. Which seat is vacant?
14. Which shoes are too large?
15. What is this place called?

LESSON VI

A. Answer the following questions both affirmatively and negatively:

1. Ist das nicht ein neuer | Anzug?
Mantel?
Hut?

2. Ist das nicht eine neue | Bluse?
Jacke?
Handtasche?

3. Ist das nicht ein neues | Kleid?
Kostüm?
Hemd?

4. Sind das nicht neue | Handschuhe?
Socken?
Strümpfe?

B. Supply the missing ending:

1. Der blau- Bleistift.
2. Mein grün- Hut.
3. Die weiß- Bluse.
4. Ein rot- Taschentuch.
5. Sein neu- Anzug.
6. Mein schön- Kleid.
7. Seine neu- Krawatte.
8. Meine braun- Schuhe.
9. Ihre gelb- Handschuhe.
10. Sind das nicht schön- Blumen?
11. Ist das nicht ein schön- Garten?
12. Hier ist unser klein- Haus.

95

C. Give the definite article and plural of: Garten, Kommode, Kind, Anzug, Dame, Schrank, Fenster, Buch, Tür, Zimmer, Baum, Blume, Löffel, Gabel, Messer, Stuhl, Kleid, Taschentuch.

D. Answer the following questions:
1. Wieviel Uhr ist es?
2. Wie heißen Sie?
3. Wo wohnen Sie?
4. Haben Sie ein Sparkassenbuch?
5. Sind Sie Deutsche(r)?
6. Bin ich Ihr Lehrer?
7. Welche Farbe hat Ihr Hut?
8. Welche Farbe haben Ihre Schuhe?
9. Wieviel Paar Schuhe haben Sie?
10. Kennen Sie meine Schwester?

E. Say in German:
1. What is your name?
2. What is your brother's name?
3. What is this flower called?
4. What is this village called?
5. It is a large village, isn't it?
6. Is this your new coat?
7. It is green, isn't it?
8. Are these your new gloves?
9. They are yellow, aren't they?
10. What colour is her new dress?
11. Isn't it a beautiful dress?
12. Isn't that an ugly big chest of drawers?

LESSON VII

A. Answer both affirmatively and negatively:

Haben Sie | einen Hund?
| eine Katze?
| ein Auto?
| einen neuen Hut?
| eine gute Feder?
| ein deutsches Wörterbuch?
| warme Handschuhe?
| große Briefumschläge?
| weiße Taschentücher?

B. Answer both affirmatively and negatively, replacing the word for *my* by the appropriate word for *your*:

Haben Sie | meinen Bleistift?
            | meine Feder?
            | mein Buch?
            | meine Streichhölzer?
            | meine Handtücher?
            | mein kleines Notizbuch?
            | meinen neuen Regenschirm?
            | meine braune Aktentasche?
            | meine weißen Briefumschläge?

C. Answer the following questions, replacing the nouns by pronouns:

1. Haben Sie mein Buch?
2. Haben Sie meine Koffer?
3. Haben Sie Karls Regenschirm?
4. Haben Sie Gretes Handtasche?
5. Nehmen Sie das Handgepäck?
6. Nimmt Ihr Vater diesen Koffer?
7. Haben Sie die Streichhölzer?
8. Hat Ihre Schwester meinen Bleistift?
9. Hat Ihr Bruder meine Aktentasche?
10. Haben Ihre Kinder unsere Wörterbücher?

D. Say in German:

1. What time is it?
2. It is half past five.
3. Is your teacher not coming?
4. He is not coming; he is ill.
5. Will you have a cup of tea?
6. I should love to.
7. Isn't it a beautiful cup!
8. I have no spoon.
9. Take my spoon.
10. I don't take sugar.
11. How many lumps of sugar do you take?
12. Have you no plate?

G

A. Turn the sentences of the Fluency Practice in Lesson VIII, 1, 2, 3, 4 and 5 into questions, and answer both affirmatively and negatively.

B. Say in German:
8.15 a.m., 9.45 a.m., 5.30 p.m., 10.05 a.m., 1.55 p.m., 12 noon, 11.35 a.m., 0.05 a.m.

C. Give the plural of:
1. Der kleine Tisch.   5. Seine rote Krawatte.
2. Mein neuer Anzug.   6. Ihr langes Kleid.
3. Dieser große Garten.   7. Unser großer Kleiderschrank.
4. Jener alte Kleiderschrank. 8. Der kleine Schlüssel.

D. Answer the following questions:
1. Ist Hamburg so groß wie Berlin?
2. Welches Land ist größer, Frankreich oder Belgien?
3. Ist der Rhein so lang wie die Donau?
4. Welcher Fluß ist länger, der Rhein oder die Themse?
5. Haben Sie so viel Geld wie Rockefeller?
6. Essen Sie gern Schokolade?
7. Was trinken Sie gern?
8. Tanzen Sie gern?
9. Gehen Sie gern ins Theater?
10. Welche Zeitungen lesen Sie gern?

E. Say in German:
1. Is that your new umbrella?
2. It is not as big as my umbrella.
3. It is smaller, isn't it?
4. I have not so many books as you.
5. You have more books than I.
6. What time is your sister coming?
7. Does she like tea?
8. What does she like to eat?
9. Do you like American cigarettes?
10. Is this the cheapest room?

Lesson IX

A. Turn the sentences under Lesson IX, 1, 3, 6 into questions. Answer them, replacing nouns by pronouns.

B. Reply to the requests of Lesson IX, 5 in the negative, replacing nouns by pronouns, e.g. *Geben Sie meinem Freund Ihre Füllfeder! Nein, ich gebe sie ihm nicht.*

C. Replace the nouns by pronouns:
1. Diese Brosche gehört meiner Mutter.
2. Dieses Haus gehört seinen Eltern.
3. Schreiben Sie Ihrem Onkel?
4. Bringen Sie die Blumen ihrer Freundin!
5. Zeigen Sie mir Ihre Füllfeder!
6. Leihen Sie uns Ihr Wörterbuch!
7. Leihen Sie meinem Bruder Ihren Bleistift!
8. Gehen Sie zu Ihren Eltern?

D. Answer the following questions:
1. Wem gehört dieses Buch?
2. Gehört Ihnen dieses Haus?
3. Essen Sie Eier zum Frühstück?
4. Essen Sie gern Rührei?
5. Gehen Sie heute zu Ihrer Tante?
6. Kommen Sie von Ihrem Onkel?
7. Schreiben Sie Ihren Eltern oft?
8. Gehen Sie heute zum Friseur?
9. Ist Ihr Bruder beim Schneider?
10. Möchten Sie eine Tasse Kaffee?

E. Say in German:
1. This belongs to me.
2. It belongs to you, doesn't it?
3. To whom do these pencils belong?
4. Are you writing to your friend?
5. I am not writing to her.
6. To whom are you writing?
7. To whom are you sending this parcel?
8. I am sending it to my friends in France.

99

9. Don't send it to them.
10. Please lend us your dictionary.
11. Where are you coming from?
12. Where are you going?

LESSON X

A. Turn the sentences of Lesson X, 2, 3, 4, 5 into questions and answer both affirmatively and negatively.

B. Insert the missing endings:
1. Das Haus unser- Eltern.
2. Die Schwester ihr- Tante.
3. Ein Geschenk sein- Onkels.
4. Die Frau unser- Lehrers.
5. Die Farbe dies- Kleid-.
6. Die Handtasche dies- Frau.
7. Die Schuhe mein- Großvaters.
8. Der Hut mein- Großmutter.

C. Insert the missing words:
1. Schreiben Sie mit—Feder.
2. Schreiben Sie nicht mit—Bleistift.
3. Sie geht mit—Kindern ins Theater.
4. Ich gehe zu—Schneiderin.
5. Wir kommen von—Großeltern.
6. Trinken Sie nicht aus—Tasse.
7. Vor—Frühstück lese ich die Zeitung.
8. Lesen Sie nicht während—Frühstücks!
9. Nach—Abendessen spielen wir Karten.
10. Ich gehe—Bäcker.
11. Er ist—Schneider.

D. Answer the following questions:
1. Schreiben Sie mit einem Bleistift oder mit einer Feder?
2. Trinken Sie Tee aus einer Tasse oder aus einem Glas?
3. Essen Sie Suppe mit einem Löffel oder mit einer Gabel?
4. Kaufen Sie Brot beim Schneider?
5. Wo kaufen wir Brot?
6. Lesen Sie die Zeitung vor oder nach dem Frühstück?
7. Lesen Sie während des Essens?
8. Trinken Sie vor der Stunde eine Tasse Kaffee?
9. Gehen Sie nach dem Abendessen spazieren?
10. Gefällt Ihnen die Farbe dieses Buches?

E. Say in German:
   1. I like your brother's tie.
   2. I don't like your sister's shoes.
   3. Do you like our teacher's hat?
   4. Do you like my friend's handbag?
   5. Can you write with this pen?
   6. I cannot drink from this cup.
   7. Are you going for a walk after the lesson?
   8. Is there a stationer's shop near here?
   9. Please give me a knife and a spoon.
   10. Please show her some note-paper.

LESSON XI

A. Answer the questions given under Lesson XI, 1, 2, 3, 5, 6 and 7.

B. Insert the missing endings:
   1. Dies sind gut- Äpfel.
   2. Haben Sie billig- Melonen?
   3. Ist dies eine gut- Ananas?
   4. Sind das nicht schön- Blumen!
   5. Haben Sie einen groß- Kasten?
   6. Haben Sie keinen größer-?
   7. Sind dies die billigst- Apfelsinen?
   8. Ist dies der best- Wein?

C. Answer the following questions:
   1. Welches ist das größte Land in Europa?
   2. Welches ist der längste Fluß in Deutschland?
   3. Wann ist es kälter, im Herbst oder im Winter?
   4. Trinken Sie gern Kakao?
   5. Was essen Sie gern?
   6. Was essen Sie lieber, einen Apfel oder eine Birne?
   7. Was trinken Sie am liebsten?
   8. Gehen Sie gern ins Kino?
   9. Wohin gehen Sie lieber, ins Theater oder ins Kino?
   10. Können Sie einen Hundertmarkschein wechseln?

101

D. Say in German:

1. How much are the strawberries?
2. Give me half a pound.
3. Are these good apples?
4. Haven't you any better ones?
5. Are these the best?
6. Are these the cheapest?
7. Haven't you any cheaper ones?
8. Do you like cold milk?
9. What do you prefer, apricots or peaches?
10. I should like a large, ripe melon.

Lesson XII

A. Turn the sentences under Lesson XII, 3 and 4 into questions and answer them (replacing nouns by pronouns).

B. Insert the missing words:

1. Stellen Sie die Flaschen auf—Tisch.
2. Wir hängen das Bild an—Wand.
3. Er steckt das Geld in—Tasche.
4. Die Stühle stehen an—Wand.
5. Stellen Sie die leeren Flaschen vor—Tür.
6. Der Koffer liegt auf—Schrank.
7. Legen Sie den leeren Koffer auf—Schrank.
8. Die Schuhe stehen unter—Bett.
9. Warum stellen Sie die Schuhe unter—Bett.
10. Die Zigaretten sind in—Kasten.

C. Answer the following questions:

1. Wo sind Ihre Kleider?
2. Wohin stellen Sie Ihre Schuhe in der Nacht?
3. Wo sind Ihre Taschentücher?
4. Womit essen Sie Suppe?
5. Woraus trinken Sie Tee?
6. Wohin gehen wir, um Shakespeares Hamlet zu sehen?
7. Wohin stellen Sie die leeren Milchflaschen?
8. Wohin legen Sie die leeren Koffer?
9. Wo haben Sie Ihr Geld?
10. Wie gefällt Ihnen das Bild an der Wand?

D. Say in German:
1. Where is my suitcase?
2. It is by the window.
3. Where shall I put the empty bottles?
4. Put them in front of the door.
5. Where are my things?
6. They are in the wardrobe.
7. Put these handkerchiefs into the chest of drawers.
8. Where is she sitting?
9. She sits by the window, between an old gentleman and a young lady.
10. Please put my armchair in front of the fireplace.

LESSON XIII

A. Change the sentences under Lesson XIII, 4, 5 and 6 into questions and answer them both affirmatively and negatively.

B. Answer the questions of Lesson XIII, 7, commencing your answer with *ich habe* . . .

C. Say in the Perfect tense:
1. Sie haben oft Besuch.
2. Ich spiele Schach (*chess*).
3. Sie raucht gern türkische Zigaretten.
4. Er trinkt kein Bier.
5. Wir lesen deutsche Zeitungen.
6. Schreiben Sie ihnen?
7. Sehen Sie ihn oft?
8. Sprechen Sie französisch?

D. Answer the following questions:
1. Wo haben Sie das Fleisch gekauft?
2. Haben Sie heute zum Frühstück Eier gegessen?
3. Was haben Sie getrunken?
4. Welche Zeitung haben Sie gelesen?
5. Haben Sie gestern Briefe geschrieben?
6. Haben Sie mich Sonntag im Park gesehen?
7. Haben Sie gestern abend ein Bad genommen?
8. Haben Sie Ihren Hausschlüssel verloren?
9. Hat Ihr Vater einen Spaziergang gemacht?
10. Hat Ihre Kusine Goethes Faust gelesen?

E. Say in German:
1. Where did you buy this umbrella?
2. Did you see your friend last night?
3. What did you do yesterday?
4. In the morning I read the newspapers and wrote some letters.
5. In the afternoon I went for a walk.
6. In the evening I listened to the wireless.
7. My wife played the piano.
8. How many hours did you work today?
9. What did you eat?
10. Did he fetch the suitcase from the station?

LESSON XIV

A. Turn the sentences under Lesson XIV, 1 and 5 into questions and answer both affirmatively and negatively.

B. Ask and answer all questions in Fluency Practice 2 and 4.

C. Change into the Perfect tense:
1. Ich gehe oft ins Theater.
2. Er kommt zu Fuß hierher.
3. Wir fahren nach Österreich.
4. Ist sie auch krank?
5. Sie bleiben sechs Wochen dort.
6. Sind Sie müde?
7. Wann kommt er zurück?
8. Wir steigen auf den Berg.

D. Answer the following questions:
1. Gehen Sie oft ins Kino?
2. Sind Sie diese Woche ins Kino gegangen?
3. Wo sind Sie gestern abend gewesen?
4. Wie lange sind Sie dort geblieben?
5. Fahren Sie im Sommer in die Schweiz?
6. Wohin sind Sie letztes Jahr gefahren?
7. Sind Sie in Österreich gewesen?
8. Sind Sie auf einen hohen Berg gestiegen?
9. Sind Sie zu Fuß hierher gekommen?
10. Um wieviel Uhr sind Sie gestern abend zu Bett gegangen?

E. Say in German:

1. Where have you been?
2. I went for a walk.
3. She stayed at home.
4. We went skating.
5. I went to the theatre on Saturday evening.
6. What did you see?
7. How did you like it?
8. I liked it very much.
9. At what time did you come home?
10. Did you walk there?
11. I was in France.
12. They went to Switzerland.

Lesson XV

A. Answer the questions under Lesson XV, 1 and 2.

B. Change into questions the sentences under Lesson XV, 4 and 7 and answer both affirmatively and negatively.

C. Say in German the following dates:
   3.5.1958, 1.6.1938, 11.1.1903, 22.12.1897, 12.3.1713, 31.8.1945, 2.11.1900, 29.2.1924, 9.10.1898, 18.5.1951.

D. Say (*a*) in the Imperfect, (*b*) in the Perfect:
   1. Er ist jede Woche hier.
   2. Sie kommt selten hierher.
   3. Sie arbeiten zu viel.
   4. Ich schreibe an unsere Freunde in Amerika.
   5. Sprechen Sie deutsch?
   6. Sehen Sie ihn?
   7. Ich gehe oft hin.
   8. Sie fahren nach Italien.

E. Say in German:
   1. We had visitors last week.
   2. My mother stayed in the kitchen.
   3. I went shopping.
   4. How long did it take?
   5. It tasted delicious.
   6. Did you ring?
   7. I waited in my room for a quarter of an hour.

8. I stayed there for three weeks.
9. We used to work in the garden.
10. We spoke German at school.
11. I found a fountain pen.
12. Did you see it?

LESSON XVI

A. Answer the questions under Lesson XVI, 3, 4 and 6.

B. Change the sentences under 5 into questions and answer them.

C. Answer the following questions:
1. Werden Sie heute ins Kino gehen?
2. Was werden Sie heute Nachmittag tun?
3. Werden Sie dieses Jahr an die See fahren?
4. Glauben (believe) Sie, daß es heute regnen wird?
5. Glauben Sie, daß es kalt sein wird?
6. Werden Sie morgen in die Schule kommen?
7. Wie lange werden Sie hier bleiben?
8. Werden Sie zu Fuß herkommen?
9. Werden Sie nächste Woche Ihre Großeltern besuchen?
10. Was werden Sie zum Abendbrot essen?
11. Wird es Wein geben?
12. Werden Sie früh zu Bett gehen?

D. Say in German:
1. It will be cold today.
2. It will rain.
3. We shall stay at home.
4. Will you go to Germany this year?
5. How long will you stay there?
6. Will you go by air?
7. I shall go by train.
8. We don't want to fly.
9. We should like to see a great deal.
10. Can one visit the castle?
11. Does one have to buy a ticket?[1]
12. Could we have breakfast early?

[1] Die Eintrittskarte, *if ticket of admission;* die Fahrkarte, *if for travel.*

APPENDIX I: DECLENSION OF ADJECTIVES AND NOUNS

Replace the first dash by any adjective and the second by any noun (there are, however, exceptions: see notes below).

	I Singular	I Plural	II Singular	II Plural
MASCULINE				
Nominative	der —e —	die —en ⸚e	ein —er —	—e ⸚e
Accusative	den —en —	die —en ⸚e	einen —en —	—e ⸚e
Dative	dem —en —	den —en ⸚en	einem —en —	—en ⸚en
Genitive	des —en —(e)s¹	der —en ⸚e	eines —en —(e)s¹	—er ⸚e
FEMININE				
Nominative	die —e —	die —en —(e)n	eine —e —	—e —(e)n
Accusative	die —e —	die —en —(e)n	eine —e —	—e —(e)n
Dative	der —en —	den —en —(e)n	einer —en —	—en —(e)n
Genitive	der —en —	der —en —(e)n	einer —en —	—er —(e)n
NEUTER				
Nominative	das —e —	die —en ⸚er²	ein —es —	—e ⸚er²
Accusative	das —e —	die —en ⸚er	ein —es —	—e ⸚er
Dative	dem —en —	den —en ⸚ern	einem —en —	—en ⸚ern
Genitive	des —en (e)s¹	der —en ⸚er	eines —en —(e)s¹	—er ⸚er

¹ Nouns of one syllable add —es, all others —s. See also note (3) below.
² Most neuters of one syllable. Others like masculine but without modification.

NOTES

(1) Adjectives preceded by *dieser, diese, dieses; jener, jene, jenes; jeder, jede, jedes; welcher, welche, welches* take the endings of Group I. Adjectives preceded by *kein(e), mein(e), dein(e), sein(e), ihr(e), unser(e), euer(e)* take the endings of Group II, but in the plural the adjective endings are the same as for Group I. Adjectives not preceded by words of either Group I or Group II have the same endings as shown for Group II with the exception of the dative and genitive, singular (see *Conversational German*, page 93).

(2) Masculine and neuter nouns ending in *–er, –el, –en,* and *–lein* have no plural endings, except *–n* in the dative.

(3) For the declension of *der Herr, der Bär, der Student, der Soldat, der Löwe* and all other masculines ending in *–e*, see page 66, Explanation 4. For irregular plural endings, see *Conversational German*, page 91.

APPENDIX II: CONJUGATION OF VERBS

REGULAR VERB STRUCTURE

Replace the dash by the stem of the verb (formed by deleting the -en or -n from the infinitive ending, e.g. *lieb-* from *lieben*).

Infinitive: –en.   Imperative: –e! –t! –en Sie!

Present Tense		Imperfect	
ich —e	wir —en	ich —(te)	wir —(t)en
du —st	ihr —t	du —(te)st	ihr —(te)t
er[1] —t	sie[2] —en	er[1] —(te)	sie[2] —(t)en

Future				Perfect[3]					
ich werde	–en	wir werden	–en	ich habe	ge–	t	wir haben	ge–	t
du wirst		ihr werdet		du hast		(en)	ihr habt		(en)
er[1] wird		sie[2] werden		er[1] hat			sie[2] haben		

[1] also *sie, es, man.*
[2] also *Sie.*

[3] Some verbs form the perfect with *ich bin, du bist, er ist,* etc. (See Lesson XIV, Explanation 1.)

Irregular verbs modify or change their root vowels: the Imperfect drops the -te and the past participle ends in -en instead of -t. The Imperative of the familiar form singular drops the -e ending: *komm! geh! schreib!*

The most frequent irregular verbs occurring in this book are *bleiben, bringen, essen, fahren, finden, geben, gefallen, gehen, kommen, lesen, nehmen, schlafen, schreiben, sehen, sein, sitzen, sprechen, trinken, tun, vergessen, verlieren.*

In the Index their principal forms are indicated in the following order: Infinitive, Imperfect, Perfect. The change occurring in the third person singular of some verbs in the Present tense is indicated in brackets after the Infinitive. Where *e* changes to *i* or *ie* the same change takes place in the second person singular, and its corresponding Imperative, e.g. *ich, sehe, du siehst, er sieht.* Imperatives: *sieh! seht! sehen Sie!* When *a* is modified this modification applies to the second and third person singular only, and not to the Imperative, e.g. *ich schlafe, du schläfst, er schläft; schlaf! schlaft! schlafen Sie!*

INDEX

The references are to pages.
(*Fluency Practice*, ordinary type; *Explanations*, **bold type**.)